GARDENS
Adirondack Style

Down East Books
Camden, Maine

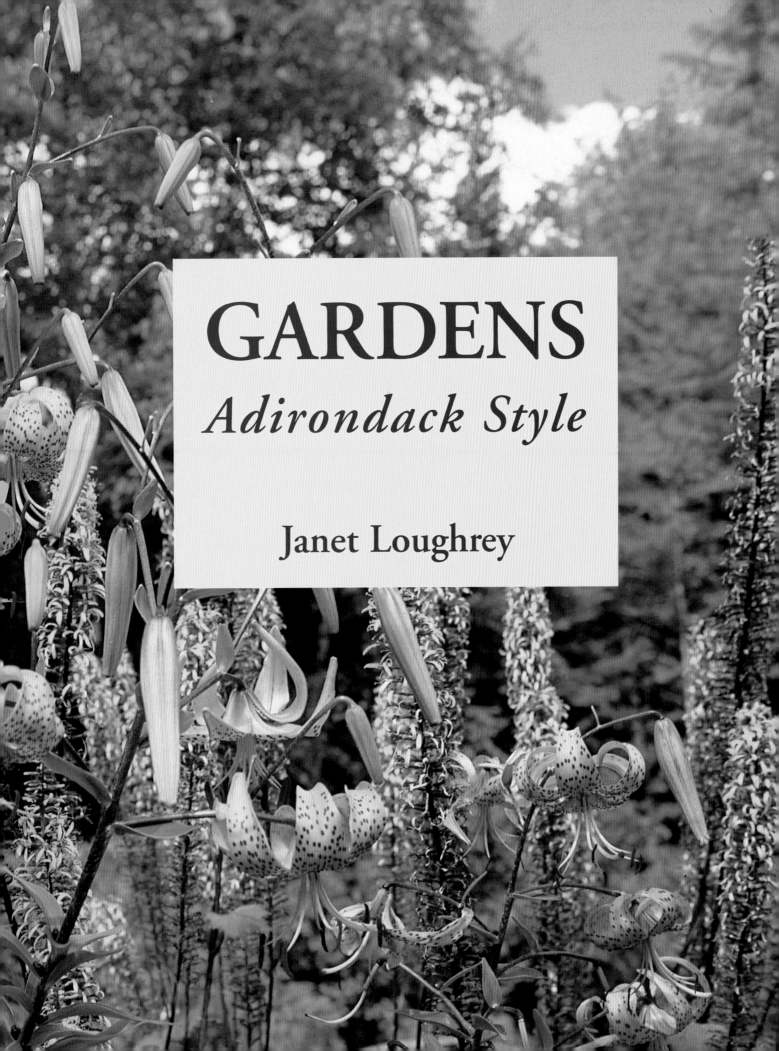

GARDENS
Adirondack Style

Janet Loughrey

To Joan Heckman and Virginia LaVaute,
who nurtured a North Country
girl's love of gardening.
And to Bryan F. Peterson,
who taught me how to see.

ISBN (10 Digit): 0-89272-623-7
ISBN (13 Digit): 978-0-89272-623-3
LCCN: 2004117294
Printed in China / OGP

2   4   5   3   1

Down East Books
A division of Down East Enterprise, Inc.,
Publisher of *Down East*, the Magazine of Maine

Book orders: 1-800-685-7962
www.downeastbooks.com

Page 1 photograph: A garden path leads visitors
into Camp Comfort

Pages 2 & 3: Tiger lily (Lilium lancifolium)*,*
globe thistle (Echinops)*, and groundsel* (Ligularia)

Right: Daylilies, purple coneflower (echinacea
purpurea)*, and gooseneck loosestrife*
(Lysimachia clethroides)

Contents

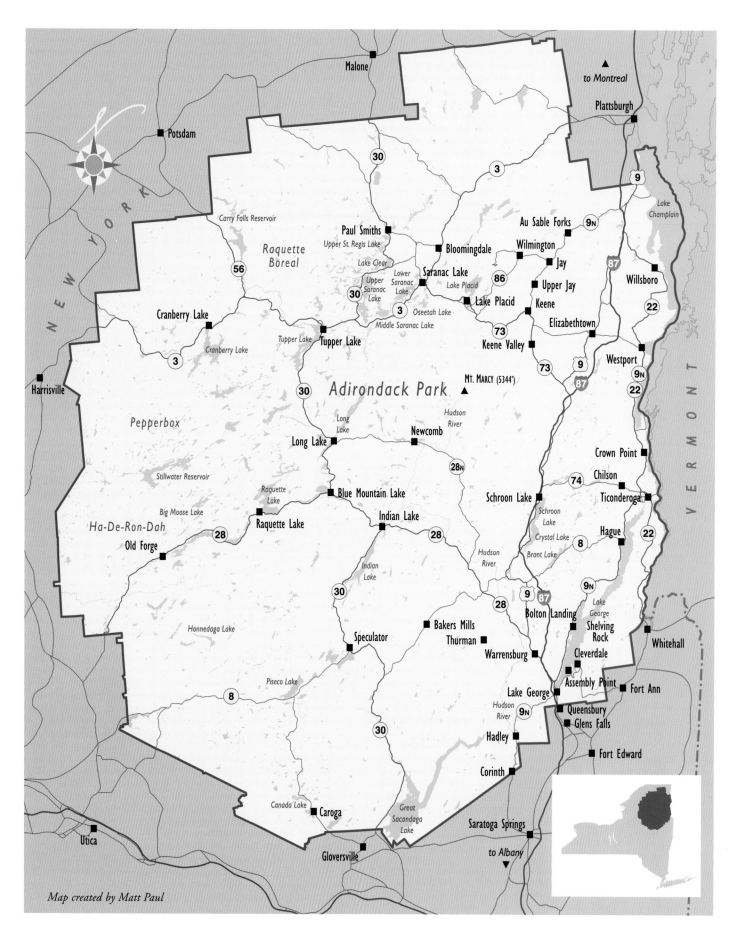

Map created by Matt Paul

hen people think of the Adirondack region of upstate New York, gardens are not the first thing that comes to mind. With a short growing season, poor soil, and interminably long winters, the Adirondack region presents a host of gardening challenges. Native tribes and early settlers labored to eke out basic sustenance from the thin, rocky soil. But gardening in the Adirondacks has been indeed alive and well—from Native American crops to kitchen and ornamental gardens of the historic Great Camps and hotels to modern-day plots of vegetables and resplendent flower borders.

New York is best known for its Manhattan skyline of towering skyscrapers and never-ending city nightlife, show tunes on Broadway, and Lady Liberty. What most outsiders don't realize is that most of New York is rural. To fly over the Empire State is to behold a crazy-quilt landscape of emerald green farmlands, gently rolling hills, quaint hamlets and villages, and, to the far north, a vast, rugged expanse of mountains, lakes, and rivers.

The Adirondack Park:
Its History, Terrain, and Climate

The Adirondack Park, in the northeastern corner of New York State, comprises an intricate patchwork of public and private lands. The six-million-acre tract is the largest wilderness area in the contiguous United States, the size of Vermont and larger than Grand Canyon, Yellowstone, Yosemite, Glacier, and Olympic National Parks combined. The park boundary is known to locals as the "Blue Line," in reference to the color used on official state maps to designate the border when the park was first created more than a hundred years ago. The jagged demarcation extends from the southern foothills near Gloversville, north to the gentle plains along the Canadian border, and east to the vast "Sixth Great Lake" that is Lake Champlain. To the west, the sparsely populated fringe boasts the exotic-sounding names of Raquette Boreal, Pepperbox, and Ha-De-Ron-Dah.

The southern boundary of the Adirondack Park is just 200 miles away from New York City, one of the most densely populated cities on Earth, yet some areas of the park are so remote that, even today, outdoor enthusiasts can go for days without seeing another person. The highest peaks in New York State are here, including forty-six summits of more than 4,000 feet. Three thousand ponds and lakes are connected by 40,000 miles of streams and rivers, the most extensive waterway in North America. The headwaters of five major rivers originate in the High Peaks region near the village of Lake Placid, site of the 1932 and 1980 Winter Olympics. The source of the mighty Hudson River is Lake Tear of the Clouds, on the upper slopes of Mount Marcy, the highest summit in New York State at 5,344 feet.

The terrain is a diverse mix of boreal wilderness, evergreen and deciduous forests, alpine tundra, and expansive meadows. More than a half-million acres of marshes and wetlands provide crucial habitat and a major migration corridor for a diverse population of birds. Forests of fir, larch, and spruce interspersed with lowland bogs and marshes characterize the boreal wilderness. The woods to the south are a mix of hardwoods (maples, beech, ash, and birch) and conifers, including the pungent balsam, whose needles are used to make aromatic pillows and sachets. The verdant forest floor is carpeted with native ferns, mosses, trillium, and the beloved lady's-slipper orchid.

The park is teeming with wildlife: white-tailed deer (all too plentiful), black bears, coyotes, beaver, fox, ermine, mink, otter, squirrels, chipmunks, lemmings, bats, and the occasional moose. A vast array of birds migrates through or stays year-round: red-tailed hawks, osprey, bald eagles, woodpeckers (including the magnificent pileated woodpecker), and songbirds. The extensive waterways are home to ducks, herons, kingfishers, geese, and the elusive common loon with its haunting call. In spring, a noisy chorus of peeper frogs fills the air with exuberant song. Although native fish populations have declined due to the effects of acid rain, the rivers and lakes are still home to trout, salmon, walleye, bass, and northern pike.

History

Tribes of Iroquois, Huron, and Algonquin Native Americans first traversed the region hundreds of years ago, hunting and fishing the bountiful forests and waterways. They seldom stayed year-round—the winters were long and harsh. The first gardens were cultivated by these natives, who grew corn, beans, and squash, known as "the three sisters." The word Adirondack is thought to be a derivation of *ha-de-ron-dah,* the Iroquois term for bark eater, in apparent belittlement of the poor farming techniques of the rival Algonquins.

Lady's-slipper orchid (Cypripedium acaule)

Frenchman Jacques Cartier was among the first explorers to see the Adirondacks; he viewed the northern edge of the mountains from atop a summit near Montreal in 1535. Samuel de Champlain sailed south from Canada on the Richelieu River in 1609 and entered the lake that would bear his name. And Henry Hudson may have glimpsed the southern Adirondack foothills in his historic journey up the Hudson River to Albany in 1608. For the next 150 years, the region went relatively unexplored except for the occasional beaver trapper or deer hunter. Decisive battles of the French and Indian Wars and Revolutionary War were waged on the eastern fringes of the vast wilderness.

Early settlers struggled to eke out a living in the harsh climate and poor soil. Large vegetable gardens were fixtures of most Adirondack homesteads. Perishable produce was dried or preserved, and more sturdy crops of potatoes, winter squash, and carrots were stored in root cellars to feed a family through the long winter months. These gardens were often planted just outside the front doorway and fenced to keep out wandering livestock.

Ornamental gardening was a luxury afforded to the wealthy, though native wildflowers and self-sowing volunteers such as hollyhocks provided a much-needed lift to the dreary, hard lives of the homesteaders. Sturdy shrubs such as lilacs were favored, because they required no work. Today, most evidence of these farming homesteads is gone, though the occasional clumps of orange daylilies, lilacs, spirea, Dutchman's pipe, or old roses that appear to grow wild in open fields or woods often mark the foundation of an old farmhouse.

The post–Civil War era was a time of newfound prosperity and unprecedented wealth. Upstart entrepreneurs invested in transportation, mining, industry, and finance, amassing seemingly unlimited fortunes. The wealthy sought leisurely respite from the large, dirty cities of Boston and New York. The close proximity of the Adirondacks and improved modes of transportation (carriages, wagons, guide boats, and steamboats) made the region a desirable destination. The undeveloped wilderness presented the wealthy the opportunity to acquire vast holdings of land. They bought up thousands of acres at a time, collectively or individually, and built grand camps and private clubs.

The natural beauty of the Adirondacks provided artistic and spiritual inspiration to poets, philosophers, composers, and painters. Naturalist Henry David Thoreau, writers Robert Louis Stevenson and John Steinbeck, Hungarian composer and pianist Béla Bartók, and painter Winslow Homer all spent time in the remote wilderness. Ralph Waldo Emerson established a "Philosopher's Camp" near Long Lake in 1857. Georgia O'Keeffe, famous for her larger-than-life floral paintings, and her husband, photographer Alfred Stieglitz, spent many summers on Millionaire's Row on the shores of Lake George. Singer and entertainer Kate Smith, best known for her rendition of "God Bless America," vacationed for thirty summers at her beloved Camp Sunshine on Lake Placid.

While the Adirondacks were being discovered and enjoyed by tourists, the great forests of pine, hemlock, and spruce were simultaneously denuded by greedy logging companies. Mountainsides were clear-cut, and erosion threatened water supplies that the southern region of the state depended upon. The ensuing public outcry resulted in the formation of the Adirondack Park. In 1894, a constitutional amendment was enacted that all forest preserve land be "forever wild," never to be sold, leased, or traded. This pioneering declaration was among the earliest and finest examples of modern-day conservation efforts.

Whereas some people were compelled to tame the wilds of the North Country for food or pleasure, others saw the Adirondacks as inspiration for creating man-made landscapes outside the region. Landscape architect Frederick Law Olmsted was so inspired with the breathtaking mountainous terrain that he designed a portion of New York City's Central Park in the image of the Adirondacks. Olmsted and his partner, Calvert Vaux, envisioned the North Woods section of the park, with its cascading streams, natural stands of trees, and rustic bridges, as a refuge for residents who could not afford to escape the urban blight. (Olmsted is best known for his visionary designs of the U.S. Capitol grounds; the campuses at Stanford, Yale, and Cornell universities; and George W. Vanderbilt's Biltmore Estate in Asheville, N.C.)

As many families settled in the Adirondacks year-round, others sought the park as a seasonal haven for recreational boating, fishing, hiking, skiing, and hunting. Throughout the twentieth century, quaint, unweatherized lakeside cottages and rustic mountain cabins were affordable even to the middle class. It was not uncommon for residents of the nearby communities of Glens Falls or Saratoga to own a second home on Lake George or points north.

Homestead garden, ca. 1910. Henry M. Beach photo, Adirondack Museum collection.

Summer residents brought divisions and cuttings of favorite plants from their year-round homes to transplant into their North Country gardens, cultivating vegetable, herb, and flower gardens during their short stays. Many wildflowers such as oxeye daisy, purple loosestrife, and yarrow growing along Adirondack roadsides are in fact cultivated varieties from Europe that escaped from these early gardens. These plants took hold in areas disturbed by farming, logging, road building, and other development.

Terrain

The Adirondack region has undergone many transformations since its tumultuous beginnings a billion years ago. Dozens of volcanoes erupted from the floor of a massive sea, rising higher than the present-day Himalayas. Over the next 500,000 years, the jagged peaks were reduced to rolling hills by the constant erosion of seawater. As the ocean receded, mile-high glaciers crept down from the north, scouring out deep valleys and great fissures. The last sheets of ice receded 10,000 years ago, shaping the present-day valleys and peaks. Melting runoff flowed into deep crevices and hollowed-out basins, creating thousands of lakes, ponds, wetlands, streams, and rivers.

The resulting terrain is an amalgam of granite outcroppings, huge boulders, and sheer rock walls soaring into the northern sky. In many places, topsoil has been completely stripped, resulting in a barren and hostile environment for plants. The highest mountain elevations are akin to the Alaskan tundra, the exposed rock faces sustaining only the toughest mosses, lichens, and alpine flowers.

The landscape of the Adirondacks has shaped the way people garden here. Granite bedrock is prevalent, so gardeners must haul in yards of nourishing topsoil to create hospitable garden beds. Soil derived from indigenous bedrock is acid and requires the addition of lime. Soil acidity or alkalinity (referred to as pH) affects a plant's ability to absorb crucial nutrients. The optimum pH—between 6 and 7 on a scale of 1 (most acid) to 14 (most alkaline)—allows beneficial microbes to thrive and plants to efficiently absorb nutrients. Bedrock-based soil is often sandy, so water and

Goldenrod near Bloomingdale

*The Hudson River
near North River*

nutrients drain through too quickly for efficient absorption. The fast drainage is ideal for plant such as heathers, but not for hellebores and hostas, which don't like to dry out. Adding compost and other organic matter provides nourishment and helps retain moisture. Acid rain, the result of airborne pollutants carried from Midwest factories and power plants, contributes to acid soil, particularly in the western region of the Adirondacks.

The Champlain Valley is decidedly different from the rest of the Adirondack Park, with gentle rolling hills and vast tracts of rich farmland. The soil comprises sedimentary limestone, resulting in an alkaline or neutral pH, and tends to be clay-based or loam. Clay soil drains poorly, inhibiting a plant's ability to absorb nutrients and causing plants to drown or rot. Adding compost, peat, and sand improves drainage and provides essential nutrients.

Climate

One of the constants in the Adirondacks is the constantly changing weather. Generations of artists have been inspired not just by the breathtaking scenery but by trying to capture the ephemeral light. Puffy white clouds sail like huge clipper ships across a blue ocean of sky, leaving a gentle wake of long, moving shadows on pastoral meadows and rugged peaks. Rays of light peek through in quick glimpses, altering the landscape in an ever-changing kaleidoscope. In a matter of minutes, these innocent-looking clouds can turn into an angry frenzy of black thunderheads, complete with deafening rumbles, hair-raising flashes of lightning, and torrents of rain or icy hail, which can rip vulnerable plants to shreds.

Ask ten Adirondackers what an "average" year of weather is like, and you'll get ten different answers. One thing is for sure: seasons in the Adirondacks are unpredictable. Long, cold winters can last for six months, the landscape dominated by lacy silhouettes of dormant trees and deep drifts of snow atop the frozen soil. In the turbulent passage from winter to spring, the freeze-thaw cycles often cause more damage to plants than the steady cold of January. When the frozen ground finally thaws for good, it turns into a quagmire of sloppy goo for a period known to locals as "mud season." The soil must dry out before being tilled or tended, testing even the most patient gardener's reserve after the interminably long winter.

Spring is short, usually no more than a few weeks. T-shirt and down-filled parka weather often occur on the same day. The early blooms of crocus, daffodils, and lilac are welcomed like long-lost friends. But just when winter seems to have loosened its icy grip, an inevitable arctic blast freezes the newly planted marigolds. Summer finally comes in earnest, and along with it the cherished blooms of peonies, Oriental poppies, and delphinium. The fleeting dog days of summer are quickly replaced by chilling night temperatures in August, and, all too soon, winter arrives again. Plants have to be tough to survive these unforgiving conditions.

The warming weather unleashes a season of a different sort: bug season. From May until August, an unrelenting succession of annoying insects makes any outdoor activity, including gardening, a challenge. Blackflies and no-see-ums cause their victims great discomfort in the warming days of spring. Close on their heels are swarms of mosquitoes and voracious deerflies. Tiny gnats in July and August work their way into ears and nostrils and underneath shirt collars. Anyone who steps outdoors likely has an arsenal of defense: long-sleeved clothing, a netted hat, and a ready supply of bug spray.

Microclimates

The United States Department of Agriculture (USDA) created a zone system of average minimum winter temperatures as a general guide to assist gardeners in determining which plants survive in their area. The scale ranges from USDA Zone 1, the coldest portion of interior Alaska, to USDA Zone 11, the breezy South Pacific tropics of the Hawaiian Islands. Most of the Adirondacks falls in USDA Zone 3 (with average minimum temperatures of –30 to –40 degrees Fahrenheit) or USDA Zone 4 (with average minimum temperatures between –20 and –30 degrees Fahrenheit).

The USDA hardiness scale is meant as a general guideline and is not the only factor to consider when selecting plants. Snow cover, elevation, and winds create varying conditions known as microclimates. Deep and consistent snow cover insulates plants from extreme cold, and gardeners can often grow plants thought to be hardy in one to two zones higher. In the USDA Zone 3 garden at the Adirondack Museum in Blue Mountain Lake, Oregon grape *(Mahonia aquifolium),* which is normally hardy to USDA Zone

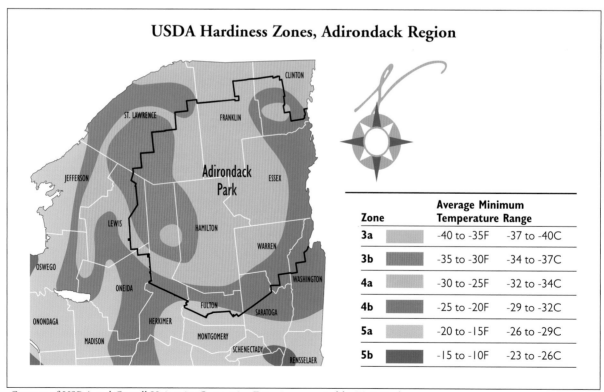

Courtesy of USDA and Cornell University Cooperative Extension, recreated by Matt Paul

Imported from Europe, the rugged orange daylily (Hemerocallis fulva) *has long been a staple of Adirondack gardens.*

5, has thrived since a summer resident planted it in the early 1900s. At Schroon Falls Farm, in the town of Schroon Lake (USDA Zone 4), David Campbell grows many USDA Zone 5 plants, siting them where the snow takes longest to melt.

The hardiness number is not an indicator of how well plants perform. Trees and shrubs that flower early in the season are susceptible to late freezes, which damage flower buds. Pagoda dogwood *(Cornus alternifolia)* and star magnolia *(Magnolia stellata)* are hardy to USDA Zone 4, yet they are rarely grown here because the flower buds are inevitably frozen by lingering frosts. In the King's Garden at Fort Ticonderoga, saucer magnolias *(M. × soulangiana)*, which are hardy to USDA Zone 5, have survived from the original garden and bloom successfully in most spring seasons. The nine-foot-tall brick wall that surrounds the garden absorbs heat and serves as a windbreak, creating a protected microclimate. Similarly, some fall bloomers such as toad lilies *(Tricyrtis hirta)* are hardy to USDA Zone 4 but bloom so late in the season that the plants are often knocked back by frost before they are able to flower.

The USDA zone map does not allow for local varia-

tions. Lake Placid, Saranac Lake, and much of Essex County, for example, are shown as being in USDA Zone 4 when, in fact, most gardens here are in USDA Zone 3. In the village of Lake Placid, the proximity to water and closeness of the buildings to one another create a moderating effect, pushing the average minimum temperatures into USDA Zone 4. Outlying areas a mile or two away can be ten degrees colder. Higher elevations as far south as Bakers Mills and Thurman are also in USDA Zone 3.

Proximity to a large body of water moderates the effects of seasonal frosts and cold winter weather. However, the lack of consistent and deep snow cover that often plagues the Lake Champlain region often negates the moderating lake effect. The Champlain Valley lies in a rain shadow, receiving less snowfall than the nearby colder High Peaks. A lower snowpack combined with desiccating winds off the lake causes plants, particularly broadleaf evergreens, to lose water through their leaves, stressing or killing the plants unless protective measures such as mulching are taken.

With the differing terrain in the Adirondacks, microclimates can vary within a small region. In low-lying areas such as Keene Valley, stationary cold air is

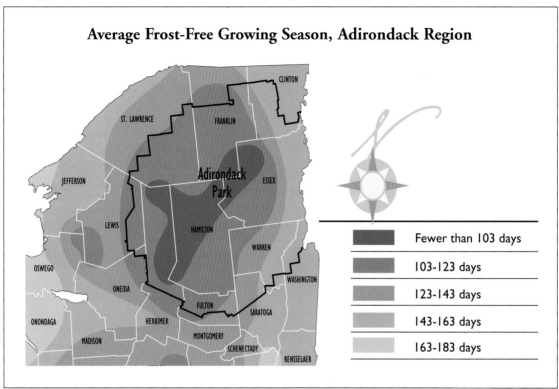

Average Frost-Free Growing Season, Adirondack Region

▓	Fewer than 103 days
▓	103-123 days
▓	123-143 days
░	143-163 days
░	163-183 days

Courtesy of Cornell University Cooperative Extension, recreated by Matt Paul

trapped, with frosts lingering longer in spring and returning sooner in fall. A nearby slope above the valley floor that receives full sun can be ten degrees or more warmer.

Microclimates occur within a single garden. Houses absorb heat during the day and release it at night, making adjacent garden beds warmer. A sunny south-facing slope can be ten degrees warmer than the shaded north side. During the dog days of summer, warm pockets may become too hot for some plants. Gardeners can take advantage of these fluctuations by siting plants in the optimum spot.

The length of the growing season varies throughout the park. The High Peaks region and other lofty elevations experience an average of 90 frost-free days a year. In some years, gardens here can experience a freeze in all twelve months. In southern areas such as Lake George, up to 150 days may be frost free in a normal year.

The USDA's average minimum temperatures have been collected from data taken over a period of many years and do not reflect short cyclical fluctuations. For much of the 1990s and early 2000s, the Adirondack region had milder winters than normal. The winters of 2002–2003 and 2003–2004 were more typical, with higher amounts of snow and colder weather. Though temperatures in these years plunged to –35 degrees Fahrenheit in Old Forge and Saranac Lake, large snowfalls in mid- to late fall insulated plants, and gardeners suffered fewer than expected losses to extreme cold.

A major killer of plants in the North Country is the dramatic freeze-thaw cycles that occur in late fall and early spring. These wild temperature fluctuations place undue stress on plants not acclimated to extreme heat or cold. Snow, organic mulches, and protective covers can help minimize damage.

Experienced Adirondack gardeners know that the secret to success is to grow vigorous plants that perform well in short-season climates. Mophead hydrangea (*Hydrangea macrophylla*) and butterfly bush (*Buddleia*) may survive some winters, but a plant whose new growth consists of no more than a couple of twigs and a few leaves is hardly the best choice.

Likewise, grafted hybrid tea roses may perform well the first year (with plenty of pampering) but will look pitiful or die altogether after a winter with −20 degree Fahrenheit temperatures. Hardy rugosa and shrub roses grown on their own roots are a much better choice. Native plants already adapted to the climate and soil conditions by virtue of evolution require little or no care once established. An Adirondack garden of native species and sturdy hybrid trees, shrubs, and perennials will not only survive but thrive.

Not surprisingly, the tried-and-true varieties that are known to thrive in the Adirondacks are found in many regional gardens. Bee balm *(Monarda)*, purple coneflower *(Echinacea purpurea)*, cinquefoil *(Potentilla)*, tickseed *(Coreopsis)*, black-eyed Susan *(Rudbeckia)*, tiger lily *(Lilium lancifolium)*, and columbine *(Aquilegia)* are just a few of the most frequently used plants. For the purposes of this book, these plants are referred to by common name only, whereas unusual cultivars and those genera that share more than one common name are referenced by both common and botanical name (genus and species, in italics).

Gardens of the Gilded Age

Those who created the elaborate ornamental gardens of the Gilded Age, from 1870 to 1910, were among the first to meet the challenges of this northern climate. With few exceptions, little was written about these late nineteenth and early twentieth century horticultural achievements, but from narrative accounts and historic photos a general picture emerges. We know that gardens and landscapes of the time were created in the European model, with neatly manicured lawns, sculpted shrubs, and stately shade trees.

Flower gardens were laid out in geometric design, with a central axis and radiating pathways. Beds were outlined with neatly pruned English boxwood, which was also used to create topiaries shaped like animals, stars, words, or patterns. Because most varieties of boxwood are marginal in the Adirondacks, barberry hedges, such as those in the King's Garden at Fort Ticonderoga, were often substituted. Korean littleleaf boxwood *(Buxus microphylla koreana)*, found at the Adirondack Museum in the village of Blue Mountain Lake, is one of only a few varieties to thrive this far north. Flower beds of the era were planted with elaborate (and usually labor-intensive) combinations of annuals and perennials in both bright and pastel color schemes.

Elaborate hardscaping consisted of stone terracing, stairways, and walls. Arbors, gazebos, and long pergolas added even more structure to these turn-of-the-century gardens. Walking paths were precisely laid out between the beds, sometimes leading into natural trails in adjoining woods or fields. Water was a recurring theme, with classic-style fountains, serene reflecting pools, and ponds filled with colorful fish. Gardens were divided into rooms by low walls and steps. Classic statuary, stone urns, gazing balls, and sundials were used as adornments. Some of the grandest gardens were those of the early resort hotels. ⁓

726. North from Ft. Wm. Henry Hotel, Fountain.

Fountain and gazing ball at the Fort William Henry Hotel. Seneca Ray Stoddard photo, Chapman Museum collection.

The period of the Industrial Revolution that followed the Civil War was a time of strong economic growth, resulting in unprecedented wealth and the acceptance of leisure activities as a legitimate pursuit. In the mid-1800s, the advent of the railroad was the major catalyst for the tourist movement in the Adirondacks. The publication of guidebooks by noted photographers Seneca Ray Stoddard and Charles S. Possons in the 1870s to 1890s introduced urbanites to the finest local resorts and the many outdoor opportunities afforded by the region.

Entrepreneurs scrambled to erect grand hotels that were architectural marvels of their time, replete with the latest amenities, including electricity and indoor plumbing. The earliest hostelries that sprang up on the shores of Lake George rivaled those in Newport, Rhode Island, and Saratoga Springs. Farther north, others were built on Schroon Lake and in the High Peaks region of Lake Placid and Saranac Lake.

A New Era of Tourism: The Grand Hotels and Resorts

In addition to fine dining, hotels offered their guests a wide variety of social, cultural, and recreational opportunities, including boating, fishing, hiking, and genteel games such as croquet, lawn tennis, and archery. Prudently situated, hotels took advantage of sites with sweeping lake and mountain vistas. The grounds were often elaborately landscaped with ornamental shrubs, trees, flowers, fountains, and walking paths. Large farms or adjacent kitchen gardens supplied food for the guests. In addition to the main farmhouse, a typical hotel farm would include a milk house, icehouse, sheep shed, brooder house, cow barn, slaughterhouse, hay barn, and other outbuildings. Many farms produced their own maple syrup.

Resort Hotels of Lake George

Fort William Henry Hotel

One of the largest and most noteworthy resorts on Lake George was the Fort William Henry Hotel, on the lake's south shore. The three-story classical-style building opened in 1854 near the ruins of Fort William Henry; it held 350 guests and was built to take advantage of the breathtaking views up the lake.

An immediate success, the hotel was quickly expanded to sleep an astounding 900 visitors. A two-story veranda looked out onto thirty acres of neatly manicured grounds that stretched from the hotel down to the lakeshore. The focal point was an enormous classical-style tiered fountain and pool. Wide gravel pathways radiated out from the fountain plaza in precise geometric formation. The grounds were planted with rare and unusual shrubs, hardwoods, and conifers. Tropical plants such as canna lilies, palms, caladiums, yuccas, dracaenas, and cactus were extremely popular during Victorian times. Some were treated as annuals; more treasured specimens were stored in heated glasshouses during the winter and placed outside each spring. A photo of the hotel's grand facade shows large circular beds planted with towering canna lilies.

After the hotel was completely destroyed by fire in 1909, a second, more modest building was erected in its place. Twenty acres of wooded park around the hotel were interconnected with gravel pathways and drives. Large elms and groupings of pines shaded large expanses of neatly clipped lawns adorned with flower beds and Italian fountains. Guests could walk through a tunnel cut in a colonnade of pungent cedars along the shore and catch glimpses of the lake through openings in the branches.

From the hotel porch, guests made their way down the gently sloping lawn along a wide gravel walk lined with flowers and ornamental shrubs. A bridge over the shore road led to a grand pergola-casino that extended over the water. The cement and marble walls were softened with bright red geraniums and trailing ivy. In this magnificent structure of porticos and archways, guests could drink, dine, and dance to a live orchestra.

Most of the second hotel was eventually razed and the entire waterfront casino was removed; a new hotel opened in 2002. Local residents recall seeing remnants of the pergola-casino as recently as the 1960s.

Gardens Along the Lake

Several other resorts on Lake George were noted for their attractive grounds. At the Fort George Hotel, the grounds were meticulously landscaped with formal walking paths, ornamental gardens, and classic arbors. Less than a mile up the lake, the Crosbyside House, which is now the site of the Wiawaka Holiday House, had a large and elaborate ornamental garden on the southeast side of its classical-style facade. In Charles Possons's guidebook, Pearl Point on Lake George is described as follows: "[The house] is nearly surrounded

Left: The original Fort William Henry Hotel. Seneca Ray Stoddard photo, Chapman Museum collection.

Below: Pergola-casino at second Fort William Henry Hotel. Jesse Wooley photo, courtesy of Henry Caldwell.

by broad piazzas, with ornamental balustrades and columns, embellished with scroll work; its beautiful shade, graded walks, verdant banks, vines and flowers display exquisite taste and ability to execute."

Farther north at the Rogers Rock Hotel, the property extended for more than a mile along the shore. Attractive flower beds were planted alongside the hotel; the natural surroundings were preserved. More than 200 rustic benches scattered about the grounds offered guests many resting points to enjoy the views of lake and mountains. A pair of elegant peacocks strutted about the grounds, lending a romantic feel. A five-acre kitchen garden supplied fresh vegetables to the hotel.

The Sagamore, Last of the Grand Adirondack Hotels

The last of the grand resorts remaining in the Adirondack Park is The Sagamore, on Green Island, near the western shore of Lake George. The island offers incomparable views looking north to The Narrows and

Northwest Bay, and south toward Dome Island. The original Queen Anne–style hostelry opened in 1883 in Bolton Landing. The grounds had expansive lawns stretching from the main buildings to the lakeshore. An extensive network of walkways lined with beautiful plantings of flowers and flanked by mature stands of pines offered respite from the hot summer sun.

The resort operated for only ten years before being

East view of The Sagamore on Lake George. Sagamore, N. Y.

Left: Postcard view of the second Sagamore Hotel. Courtesy of Hugh Allen Wilson and Marshall Ford.

Right: Aerial view of the present-day Sagamore Resort on Green Island

destroyed by fire in 1893. A second, more modern building erected on the original foundation was opened the following year. Except for a few stands of birch, hemlock, and pine, the landscaping had been ravaged by the fire, so new trees, shrubs, and flowers were added. Wide, formal walkways were covered with tanbark, a mulch made from hemlock bark (the "tan" referring to tannic acid), and formal circular beds were filled with colorful flowers. Guests could relax and enjoy tea on the outdoor terraces overlooking the waterfront gardens. A full staff of gardeners kept the grounds immaculately maintained. Large glass greenhouses were used to start vegetables, which supplied food for the hotel, and to protect tender flowers from early-season frosts.

The second Sagamore hotel survived twenty years before succumbing to fire in 1914. With the advent of World War I, plans for a new hotel were delayed.

The present Colonial Revival building was finally opened in 1922. Over the next several decades, the resort would experience various ups and downs. Under new ownership in the 1980s, The Sagamore was revived into one of the premier resorts in the northeastern United States. The hotel was completely remodeled, and a conference center, sports facilities, several restaurants, and condominium units were added. A former carriage house was renovated into eleven two-story suites, each with its own private garden. An elaborate design by L. A. Partnership landscape architects in Saratoga utilized more than 200 varieties of native and ornamental shrubs, perennials, and annuals.

Today, the grounds are fabulously landscaped with colorful perennial borders and established plantings of ornamental shrubs and shade trees. A large circular flower bed with a fountain in the center greets visitors as they arrive at the main hotel. Yellow-flowered

black-eyed Susan, tickseed, and lady's mantle *(Alchemilla mollis)* are complemented by purple coneflower, iris, and gayfeather. Soft pink phlox, apricot-colored daylilies, blue delphinium, and white daisies offer additional contrast.

The front of the conference center is lavishly planted with colorful annuals and perennials that bloom profusely all summer and fall. Annual baby's breath *(Gypsophila)*, impatiens, fan flower *(Scaevola aemula)*, and Wave Hybrids petunias fill in the gaps around repeat-blooming daylilies, tickseed, primrose, speedwell, and salvia, all known for their long flowering times.

A grand promenade flanked by formal-style flower beds runs from the front veranda of the hotel down to the wharf, where guests once arrived by steamboat. A large pond complete with a waterfall and statuary was recently constructed near the renovated carriage house. Locals and hotel guests alike come to relax and enjoy the gardens.

Above: Flower bed and fountain at the entrance to the hotel at Sagamore

Below: Long-blooming perennials and annuals at the entrance to the resort's conference center

Resorts of Schroon Lake

Schroon Lake, twenty-five miles north of Lake George Village, was once known as a miniature Switzerland. Smaller and less developed than Lake George, the region has retained much of its natural beauty. In the late 1800s, several resorts thrived and prospered well into the twentieth century.

The Brown Swan Club and Word of Life

The Brown Swan Club, opened in 1916, was a private resort located south of the village of Schroon Lake. The club's motto was "Large enough to be excellent, small enough to be personal." A 1920s pamphlet reads, "A special feature is the table supplied with fresh vegetables from our own garden; eggs, chickens and milk from the Club farms." One pamphlet photograph shows a long pergola extending out from the main building. Other photos reveal that the grounds were richly landscaped with trees, shrubs, and flowers.

In 1953, Brown Swan was sold to Word of Life, a Christian organization, which opened the club as a retreat. By then, the grounds were in disarray and Chris Williams was hired to spruce up the property; he was employed until 1968. According to Harry Norman, who has tended the gardens since 1971, there is still

Above: The grounds at the Brown Swan Club. Courtesy of Schroon–North Hudson Historical Association.

Below: Hydrangeas overlooking the lake at Word of Life, site of the former Brown Swan Club

evidence of the original stone edging of the formal flower beds and brick walking paths.

Today, the grounds at Word of Life are fabulously landscaped with massed plantings of colorful annuals. The shaded woodland setting is also home to reliable hostas, ferns, peegee hydrangeas, and other

sturdy shrubs. Norman created most of the gardens, including several whimsical elements. "Word of Life" and other phrases are spelled out in shaped ground covers along the front of the bookstore. A large working clock near the main building is set into a grassy knoll and planted with ground covers and

Above: The grounds at Word of Life are richly landscaped with large beds of annuals and sturdy perennials.

Right: Brightly colored annual impatiens and coleus planted among reliable hostas light up a shaded woodland area.

marigolds and other annuals. (The hands and numerals are the only parts of the clock that can be seen; the mechanism itself is not visible.) Tiers of petunia baskets placed around the grounds resemble blooming trees.

The main building is now the Word of Life Inn. Where the long rose pergola once stood, a brick seating area is decorated with annual salvia, geranium, sweet potato vine, sweet alyssum, petunias, and spiky dracaena along a low stone wall of river rock. Between the inn and the lake, a circular fountain is surrounded with hosta. Under a canopy of pines, adjacent beds are planted with brightly colored coleus and impatiens. At the entrance, "Welcome" is spelled out in sculpted ground covers surrounded by long beds of petunias with a backdrop of peegee hydrangeas.

A working clock at Word of Life is planted with a meticulous tapestry of anual flowers and groundcovers

Leland House

The first Leland House, located in the center of the village of Schroon Lake, was an elegant Victorian showpiece. Its grand piazza looked out onto six acres of neatly manicured grounds extending from the hotel down to the lakeshore. The expansive lawns were planted with a wide variety of evergreens, tall shade trees, and ornamental shrubs. Comfortable walking paths encouraged visitors to stroll along the formally edged flower beds. Along the pathways strollers encountered the occasional decorative fountain, arbor, or gazebo.

The hotel burned to the ground in 1914 and was quickly replaced in 1915 with a Colonial Revival–style building. Historical illustrations suggest that the grounds were landscaped in the same style. A nearby farm supplied vegetables, milk, butter, eggs, and poultry to the hotel kitchen. Cut flowers were grown to decorate the public rooms and dining tables.

The second hotel burned in 1938; the Schroon Lake Town Park now occupies the site.

The second Leland House, ca 1920. Postcard lithograph, Adirondack Museum collection.

Taylor House and Scaroon Manor

In 1885, Charles and Sarah Taylor built the Taylor House on the west side of the lake, approximately five miles south of Schroon Lake village. It was small compared to the grand hotels of Lake George, consisting of a main building with eighteen sleeping rooms, fifteen cottages, and various outbuildings. A brochure from the early 1900s shows a long, shaded walkway by the lake and formal flower beds around the hotel and cottages. The grounds are described in the brochure as "two hundred acres . . . [with] frontage on Schroon Lake of a little over a mile. . . . Fifty acres are under a high state of cultivation, furnishing fresh vegetables, etc. in abundance."

The Taylor House was rebuilt in 1925 and renamed Scaroon Manor. Known for its gay social scene and live entertainment, the resort was popular with up-and-coming stars from New York City. Red Skelton made some of his earliest appearances here. Nightly performances of comedy, drama, and musical revues took place in an outdoor amphitheater with a revolving stage. This vacation spot was one of the first to cater to those of the Jewish faith, providing guests with a rabbi to conduct services for Passover and other holy days. The resort is best known as the setting for the 1958 movie *Marjorie Morningstar*, starring Natalie Wood and Gene Kelly.

The lavishly landscaped grounds were the pride of Scaroon Manor. Terraced gardens stretched from the hotel, alongside the amphitheater, and down to the lakeside sports courts, where guests could partake in tennis, handball, and roller skating. Formal, round beds were connected by wide walking paths that encircled each garden. The paths were outlined with neatly clipped hedges and surrounded by lush green lawn. Tall evergreens provided occasional vertical accents. Produce for the table was grown in two large vegetable gardens—one along the lake near the boathouses and a larger plot behind the main house.

A pamphlet shows lush flower beds by the archway entrance to the main house. An outdoor patio adjacent to an elegant fountain featured rustic log benches surrounded by flowers and shrubs. In an updated brochure, the resort is described as "Nature's natural

Scaroon Manor promotional brochure. Adirondack Museum collection.

'Heaven on Earth,' . . . Beautifully landscaped grounds; pine tree lined walks; velvety turf garlanded with thousands of exotic flowers and shrubs; form an appropriate setting for the jewel that is Scaroon."

But the jewel lost its luster, and in the 1960s, the property was sold to the state of New York. The buildings were demolished and the gardens abandoned. Remnants of the gardens today suggest a diverse palette of shrubs, trees, and flowers. A long allée of peegee hydrangeas and lilacs most likely greeted visitors who entered down the long driveway. A hedge of highbush blueberries was planted along the road as screening. The outline of the formal gardens near the

amphitheater can still be seen; there are vestiges of German and flag irises, daylilies, tiger lilies, barberries, Peking cotoneasters, and various bulbs. Along the verandas, Dutchman's pipe vines were most likely trained on trellises, as they are commonly used now. The site is being converted into a day-use park.

Although the buildings of Scaroon Manor were torn down in the 1960s, vestiges of the amphitheater and projection room, as well as fountains and other adornments, remained. In 1971, the Adirondack Mountain Garden Club purchased one of the large Italianate fountains and its stone basin from the town of Chester for a nominal fee. The town moved the

Postcard views of the Scaroon Manor amphitheater (top) and park (bottom). Courtesy of Nancy Harste.

A welcome garden in the town of Chester features a fountain and shrubs from the gardens of the now-defunct Scaroon Manor.

fountain a few miles south to an intersection on Route 9 near Northway Exit 26. With a permit from the state of New York, the garden club rescued surviving shrubs from the Scaroon Manor gardens. The fountain and plants are now the centerpiece of a welcome garden, where visitors can enjoy a small piece of a lost era.

Resorts of the High Peaks Region

The Stevens House

The High Peaks region, from the Keene Valley to Saranac Lake, became a popular tourist destination because of its dramatic views of the state's tallest mountains. The Stevens House, built on Signal Hill, between Lake Placid and Mirror Lake, was a well-known local landmark for more than fifty years. Originally opened as a hotel in 1855 by farmer Joseph V. Nash, it was renamed when the property was sold to John A. Stevens.

A fire destroyed the building in 1885; a new hotel opened in 1886, eventually becoming the largest in Lake Placid, accommodating five hundred guests.

According to an 1889 pamphlet on the new Stevens House, "Two hundred acres . . . are under cultivation as a farm and garden, which supply an abundance of fresh vegetables, eggs, butter, cream, milk and cheese." A series of flower beds adjacent to the hotel were

arranged with a circular garden in the center and triangular or crescent-shaped beds radiating out from the center. Farther down the gentle slope was a large vegetable garden laid out in orderly rows.

After several expansions and remodelings, as well as closures during the Great Depression and World War II, the hotel was demolished in 1947.

The Saranac Inn

Located ten miles west of Lake Placid, the Saranac Lakes region was popularized for its many interconnected lakes and ponds. The largest, Upper Saranac Lake, was the location of many private camps and several public hotels. The Saranac Inn, one of the largest and most luxurious resort hotels in the Adirondacks, was situated on a peninsula at the northern end of Upper Saranac Lake. The site commanded arresting mountain and lake vistas. The hotel, opened in 1864, was called Prospect House. In 1886, after expanding and changing hands several times, it was renamed Saranac Inn.

An improved railroad route in 1892 made travel to the region easier and faster, and the area quickly became a vacation destination for such notable figures as Theodore Roosevelt, Grover Cleveland, and the Rockefeller family. By the prosperous 1920s, the Saranac Inn had reached its peak capacity—an astounding one thousand guests. Like other resorts of the time, the inn was a self-sufficient complex containing barns, stables, a carpenter shed, blacksmith shop, woodshed, laundry, meat market, an icehouse, and a general store. A map of the grounds shows a large garden directly east of the inn, with a gardener's cottage to the side. The plot was laid out in long, neat rectangular beds with evenly spaced rows and wide pathways. The lush kitchen gardens were planted with a vast array of flowers, herbs, and vegetables.

Wawbeek Lodge

Just a few miles to the south, the Wawbeek Lodge was built in the mid-1880s on the western shore of Upper Saranac Lake. The hotel was quickly expanded to accommodate a hundred guests, and the grounds were richly landscaped to accentuate the incomparable views. Young shade trees were planted in straight rows alongside the formal flower beds, which extended down the gentle slope to the water's edge. The neatly manicured lawn was traversed with walking paths. The beds were crisply edged with small hedging and filled with colorful annuals. Lush vines softened the lattice and railings of the wraparound verandas; the vines reached to the second story.

By 1914, the lodge (now called the Hotel Wawbeek) was unable to remain profitable and was forced to

A postcard of the Stevens House shows adjacent ornamental and vegetable gardens. Adirondack Museum collection.

The grounds and lawn at Wawbeek Lodge. Henry M. Beach photo, ca. 1912, courtesy of the Bogdan Collection.

THE WAWBEEK LAWN.   WAWBEEK.N.Y.

close. The buildings were torn down and a smaller hotel was built in 1922. It burned following the 1980 Winter Olympics in Lake Placid; an annex of rustic log buildings remains today and is operated as an upscale resort, called The Wawbeek on Upper Saranac Lake.

After World War II, middle-class America became more mobile with the widespread use of the automobile. Many of the grand hotels that remained were torn down to make way for economy motels and cottages, and an era of elegant living was over. ❧

Looking to the Wawbeek boathouse and Upper Saranac Lake. Henry M. Beach photo, ca. 1912, courtesy of the Bogdan Collection.

*T*he Gilded Age, from the end of the Civil War until World War I, was an era of great affluence; the newly wealthy had both the means and the time for leisure and social pursuits. Many were content to spend their summers at popular tourist destinations such as Lake George; others ventured farther north into the park, seeking adventure and solitude. Railroad magnate William West Durant built the first "Great Camp" on Raquette Lake in the 1870s. He persuaded many prosperous families, including the Rockefellers, Carnegies, Morgans, and Vanderbilts, to follow suit.

Although the wealthy proved eager to get away from it all, they were not anxious to leave luxury behind. Their rustic camps were extensive compounds of a half dozen to more than fifty buildings that included a main house, guest cottages, servants' and gardeners' quarters, living and recreational buildings, and vast kitchens and food pantries. Despite the remoteness of the region, owners continued their lavish social lifestyle, hosting soirees rivaling even the most elegant Manhattan affair.

Gardens of the Great Camps

Elaborate attention to detail and fine craftsmanship utilizing wood and stone gave birth to the Adirondack style of architecture. The use of indigenous raw materials such as rough-hewn logs, uncut rock, and locally mined iron allowed the buildings to harmonize with their surroundings. Fine antique furniture brought from the cities was replaced by rustic pieces made from twigs and branches by local artisans. The rugged surroundings were compensated for by the latest amenities, including electricity, running water, and indoor bathrooms. Later, the Great Camps had movie projection rooms, bowling alleys, heated cloakrooms, and photo darkrooms.

Because outside sources of food, services, and supplies were inconsistent and scarce, the camps were run as self-sufficient entities, with enormous staffs of caretakers, cooks, maids, butlers, valets, chauffeurs, gardeners, farmhands, blacksmiths, carpenters, painters, laundresses, and seamstresses. Most camps had their own farms with livestock and plots that provided food for the staff and guests. Extensive kitchen and cutting gardens supplied fruits, vegetables, and fresh flowers for the table. Glass hothouses were used to grow annual, perennial, and vegetable seedlings and even fabulous tropical orchids.

Early spring in the main garden at Camp Rivermouth

Camp owners spent just two to three months in summer at their rustic retreats. During the rest of the year, there were still many chores to be done. In spring, the gardens and fields were cleared, tilled, and planted. Come summer, the farm, gardens, and lawns were tended in preparation for the owners' arrival. Wild berries were picked from nearby woods and fields and preserved for jams and jellies. In fall, garden produce was harvested, canned, and stored, mostly for use by the staff, while the rest was consumed by the owners and their guests during their short summer sojourns.

William West Durant's prototype, Camp Pine Knot on Raquette Lake, signified not only the beginning of Adirondack architecture but an entire lifestyle of "roughing it" in comfort. Durant spent fifteen years dabbling with various construction techniques and building styles. Elements of primitive log cabins, Native American wigwams, and Iroquois longhouses were combined with attributes of the Swiss chalets that Durant admired while traveling in Europe. With Japan's recent opening to the West, Far Eastern ornamentation was the rage; pagodas, teahouses, lanterns, and arched bridges were used to decorate many of the Great Camps.

The challenge of gardening at Durant's first camp is described in the August 25, 1900, issue of *The Mail and Express Illustrated Saturday Magazine:* "The preserve comprises many hundreds of acres, much of it virgin forest, where deer was [sic] so plentiful that it was found necessary to protect the camp garden plot by high wire fences, to save the growing vegetables from their depredations." The article further describes old-fashioned morning glories growing in great profusion throughout the camp.

Great Camp Gardens of a Lost Era

Kamp Kill Kare

Kamp Kill Kare, located on an isolated private lake near Raquette Lake, was part of Durant's original holdings and is one of the finest examples of Great Camp architecture, with elaborate rustic furnishings, log beams, twig embellishments, and massive stone fireplaces. Still privately owned, the camp is also one of the best preserved.

Early photos show a large vegetable and flower garden with two glass greenhouses and an adjacent garden shed. Farm buildings constructed from 1915 to 1917 were built of cyclopean stone, a style of construction using large, irregular cut blocks assembled without mortar. A five- to six-foot-high fence encircling the plot discouraged marauding deer. Some beds were laid out in crescent shapes, with neatly trimmed edges and wide pathways in between. Others were shaped in small circles, triangles, and even a star, which was fashionable at the time. The modern-day camp is said to have magnificent ornamental gardens.

Gardens, greenhouses, and gardener's cottage at Kamp Kill Kare, ca. 1914. Henry M. Beach photo, Adirondack Museum collection.

Sagamore

One of the crowning masterpieces of all Great Camps is the Sagamore Lodge, located on a small, private lake near the hamlet of Raquette Lake. Built by Durant after the early camps of Pine Knot, Camp Uncas (owned by J. P. Morgan), and Kamp Kill Kare, the Swiss chalet–style lodge is a defining example of grand rustic architecture.

The property was purchased in 1901 from Durant by Alfred Gwynn Vanderbilt, grandson of Commo-

dore Vanderbilt, one of the country's wealthiest men.

The farm and outbuildings at Sagamore were far more extensive than those of previous camps, with several livestock barns for cows, chickens, and pigs. A root cellar made of cut stone was used to store potatoes, onions, carrots, and winter squash. Between the farm buildings and main lodge was a three-acre garden for vegetables and flowers, enclosed by a high wire fence to keep out deer. At the center was a large, circular bed of flowers. Four pathways radiated at

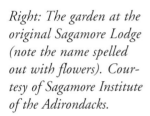

Right: The garden at the original Sagamore Lodge (note the name spelled out with flowers). Courtesy of Sagamore Institute of the Adirondacks.

Below: The present-day main lodge at Sagamore Great Camp

ninety-degree angles from the center; each symmetrical bed was formally planted. As was fashionable, "Sagamore Lodge" was spelled out with flowers in eight-foot-high letters. A glass greenhouse protected vegetable and flower seedlings. The small triangular plot where two roads intersected was dedicated to a stand of cheerful sunflowers, grown separately from the main garden. On the opposite side of Sagamore Lake were fields of corn and potatoes.

The Sagamore has a happier ending than many of the Great Camps. It was restored and is now owned and operated as a lodge by the nonprofit Sagamore Institute of the Adirondacks. It is open for guided tours from May through October.

Profile of an Adirondack Camp Gardener

Some of the old camps were family-run hunting and fishing retreats where tourists could experience the rustic lifestyle of the Adirondacks in relative comfort. The jobs of maintenance, guides, and gardeners were often filled by colorful characters who eschewed the traditional nine-to-five routine.

At Higby Resort on Big Moose Lake, head gardener Mr. Batty (whose first name is unknown) was adept at maintaining the five-acre vegetable plot that provided fresh produce for guests and staff. His specialties were plump, juicy strawberries and the rich golden honey that he harvested from carefully maintained beehives.

Mr. Batty, whose long, thick beard partially hid his toothless grin, enjoyed his drink and told wild tales of his alleged adventures of fighting off grizzly bears while delivering mail for the Pony Express. He was the butt of many jokes for his unsuccessful attempts at keeping deer out of the vegetable garden.

Henry M. Beach photo, ca. 1912. Courtesy of Bogdan Collection.

Camp Inman

Although most Great Camp plots were dedicated to providing food for the table, some camp owners designed gardens for ornamental pleasure. Horace Inman, a manufacturer and inventor from Amsterdam, New York, purchased the four-acre Round Island on Raquette Lake in the 1890s. Its camp consisted of thirty-five modest wood-frame buildings with cedar siding; the main lodge was insulated for year-round use with raw cork imported from Portugal. The architectural style was heavily influenced by Inman's trips around the world, particularly the Orient. Bamboo, statuary, and other adornments from China and Japan were shipped to the Adirondacks, where they were used to decorate the camp.

Inman had a particular fondness for growing plants. He raised exotic tropicals in a large glass greenhouse heated by steam pipes. A floating Japanese pagoda was built on log pontoons at the edge of the lake. The wooden "tea house," as it was known, was decorated with fine silks and linens and sparsely furnished with floor mats; guests were asked to remove their shoes

Above: Teahouse at Camp Inman, ca. 1890. Adirondack Museum collection.

Below: Horace Inman in his camp garden, ca. 1890. Adirondack Museum collection.

before entering. A remarkable flower and vegetable garden enclosed by logs was built adjacent to the pagoda on a large, floating platform on the lake. Because the island is rocky with little topsoil, it's possible that this was thought of as a practical solution.

Elegant peacocks that strutted freely about the island were part of a bird aviary. A series of cascading Japanese-style fountains was powered by a steam pump that supplied the camp's water from the lake. The central fountain was shaped like a lily with a dragon spouting water from its mouth, surrounded by three smaller tiers.

The camp, still owned by the Inman family, now consists of several buildings, including one recently constructed. There are still a few remnants of the garden, including the pilings on which the tea house once rested, the base of the large fountain, and one or two original urns.

Santanoni

One of the most extensive of all Great Camp farms was Santanoni, located in Newcomb, south of the High Peaks region. The vast complex of buildings and farms on 12,500 acres was completed in the early 1890s. The first owners were Robert Pruyn, a successful businessman from Albany, and his wife, Anna. The camp was built in three separate locations. The gatehouse complex, with a massive stone entrance,

staff quarters, and other outbuildings, was situated at the edge of the town of Newcomb. A mile farther into the estate was the farm; the final complex was the main camp, located on Newcomb Lake.

The two-hundred-acre farm was three and a half miles from the main camp on a south-facing slope with views of Vanderwhacker Mountain. The ambitious complex consisted of many barns, four houses for the garden staff, a creamery, chicken coops, a slaughterhouse, a smokehouse, kennels, a seed house, and a root cellar. Large populations of chickens, sheep, cattle, goats, and pigs supplied food for the camp. Surplus dairy products were sold to residents of Newcomb. A half-acre vegetable garden was enclosed by an eight-foot-high fence to keep out deer. Concrete hotbeds covered with glass retained warmth from the sun, giving tender seedlings a head start in the short season.

In 1953, the Pruyns sold the camp to the Melvin family, who kept it for almost twenty years. The land was eventually sold to the state of New York and became part of the State Forest Preserve. Today, the buildings at Santanoni Preserve, as it is now called, are being restored in cooperation with the Adirondack Architectural Heritage (AARCH) and the town of Newcomb. The land is open to hikers, skiers, hunters, and horseback riders; several annual tours are offered through AARCH.

Santanoni farm. Adirondack Museum collection.

White Pine Camp

In 1926, the tiny hamlet of Paul Smiths was thrust into the national spotlight when President Calvin Coolidge elected to spend his summer vacation there. The president and his wife were guests of the Kirkwood family, longtime friends who owned White Pine Camp on Osgood Pond. For ten weeks beginning in early July, all national business was conducted from the remote "Summer White House."

The compound, unique for its fusion of modern and rustic styles, was built in classic Great Camp style, with separate buildings that housed a living room, a dining hall and kitchen, staff quarters, guest cabins, a pump house, an icehouse, and even a bowling alley. The buildings were constructed with unconventional (not 90-degree) wall angles, soaring rooflines, skylights, and a new style of siding. Manhattan-based architect William Massarene had planned to use clapboard siding, but Benjamin Muncil, a skilled local builder, preferred traditional Adirondack log design. They settled on a compromise developed by Muncil and local millwright Charles Nichols—rough-hewn boards with an untrimmed bottom edge they named "brainstorm" siding, perhaps because of the collaboration involved. The siding is also known as "Adirondack" and became popular in other camps throughout the region.

One of the unique features of White Pine Camp is a hundred-yard-long floating wooden footbridge that extends from the lakeside boathouse across a lagoon. At the end of the boardwalk is a man-made island with an arching Japanese-style bridge and a wood-frame teahouse. On a misty early morning, the view across the water to the teahouse framed by windswept pines is reminiscent of an ancient Oriental painting.

The grounds were beautifully landscaped; impressive plantings of old rhododendrons can be found on the property, their size and sturdiness unusual this far north. A full-time gardener was kept on staff year-round and provided with his own separate quarters. Two glass greenhouses protected tender flower and vegetable seedlings in early spring. Large pots and stone urns adorning the grounds were replanted with fresh flowers every two weeks. There are still remnants of the original alpine rock garden, where Mrs. Coolidge was reportedly fond of strolling each morning. In a *New York Times Magazine* article dated August 1,

1926, and titled "Mr. Coolidge Is Learning to Play," writer Charles R. Michael says, "Sometimes she [Mrs. Coolidge] walks as far as the lodge gates, where there is an Alpine rock garden containing sixty-three varieties of Alpine and wild flowers, a garden pronounced by experts as one of the most complete of its kind."

Several years after Coolidge's legendary visit, the camp changed hands and was eventually given to Paul Smith's College. The property was resold and purchased by a private group of individuals who began a process of historic preservation. Cabins are available for year-round rentals, and the grounds are open on a limited basis for small tours. There are several new perennial gardens around the main complex, and containers and flower beds are planted with colorful annuals.

In 2004, several of the camp's owners uncovered the alpine garden, which was overgrown by weeds, brush, and trees. Using historic accounts and records, they plan to restore the garden to its original splendor.

Contemporary Camp Gardens

Many Great Camps suffered demise by fire or a slower death by decay and neglect. Some have been kept in the same family for generations; others were preserved and restored to their former glory by those with the means and appreciation for this lost lifestyle.

Camp Woodmere

At Camp Woodmere on Upper St. Regis Lake, an extensive compound of small outbuildings rims a naturally bowl-shaped amphitheater. The camp, built in 1883, was purchased by the present owner's family in 1888. In true Great Camp style, there are numerous (in this case, twenty-six) buildings. The main cabin consists of a living room, a dining room, a kitchen, and a master bedroom. Outbuildings include sleeping cabins, guides' and servants' quarters, an icehouse, and two boathouses.

The original gardens consisted of naturalized wildflowers and native woodland plants. By 1997, when the grounds became untidy and overgrown with weeds, landscape designer Janine Taylor removed the wildflowers and began renovating the garden beds. Rock terraces were built to retain the soil along the steep slope, and loads of rich compost and other nutrients were added to the existing soil. The soil underneath the tall stands of hemlock dries out quickly, so Taylor uses plants that can readily adapt. Fallen needles make the soil acid, so lime is generously applied each year.

A dense evergreen canopy was thinned to allow more light. Native ferns were collected from the surrounding woods and planted into a lovely fern grotto at the north side of the amphitheater. With the garden now receiving more sunlight, other perennials have adapted well to the forest setting. The gently sloping terraces are planted with sturdy daylilies, black-eyed Susan, wild ginger (*Asarum europaeum*), Shasta daisy, and native grasses.

Peak color is planned for July and August, when the camp is most visited. When planting a new area, Taylor starts with gallon-size specimens or larger, and plants early in the season so they have time to develop a deep root system, giving them a better chance of

Facing page: The hillside gardens at Camp Woodmere

Right: Stone terracing helps retain topsoil in sloping beds.

Below: A glen of naturalized ferns flanks one of Camp Woodmere's shaded lawns.

surviving the deep freeze of the subsequent winter.

Deer are frequent visitors, so Taylor includes a selection of deer-resistant plants: perennial catmint *(Nepeta)*, bee balm, butterfly weed *(Asclepias tuberosa)*, monkshood, and salvias. The sharp thorns of barberry shrubs and rugosa roses are also deterrents to four-legged marauders. Like other gardeners, Taylor has found that the odor of Milorganite fertilizer seems to repel deer, though this is not a proven scientific fact. The slow-release organic amendment is safe for lawns, ornamentals, and edibles and resists leaching, making it a good choice for sandy soils.

Three Timbers

Near the hamlet of Paul Smiths, an overpopulation of white-tailed deer competes for limited food sources. A lovingly tended garden can be decimated in a single day by a hungry herd. At Three Timbers, on the edge of a private pond, the solution was to enclose the garden with a deer-proof cedar structure. The homeowner wanted a serene, contemplative space where family and guests could linger and enjoy the private seating areas, soothing water features, and colorful display of plants. The challenge for designer Peter Fry was to construct a fence that was both attractive and functional.

Through meticulous research and practical trial and error, Fry determined that irregular openings no greater than ten inches by two feet would deter most deer. The fence was built seven feet tall above a two-foot-high foundation of sandstone mined from a quarry near Malone. The fortified cedar enclosure complements the home's fusion of Great Camp and Japanese architecture and blends with the surrounding woods.

A double-seated gazebo serves as the garden's entrance. The corner posts, arranged in groupings of three, reflect the sacred Trinity theme found throughout the camp. Fry designed the interconnected series of bubbling fountains and pools to emulate the surrounding landscape of ponds and streams. Flagstone pathways rim a subtle centerpiece sculpture of moss-covered boulders. Crispin Shakeshaft of The Munson Group, Inc., was involved with many aspects of the construction, collecting, curing, and installing the cedar posts and building the gazebo and benches.

The planting design was created by Fry and installed by Janine Taylor, who continues to maintain the gardens. An eclectic mix of bulbs, annuals, and perennials

Practical as well as dramatically ornamental, the fence at Three Timbers keeps hungry deer out of the garden.

provides color from spring to fall. In summer, reliable perennials including gayfeather, peonies, catmint, Oriental lilies, phlox, and pincushion flower *(Scabiosa)* bloom in a progressive sequence of color. The taller backdrop includes ligularia, globe thistle, and bugbane *(Actaea simplex* 'Brunette', formerly *Cimicifuga simplex)*. A riotously colored display of annual dahlias, cosmos, petunias, lantana, and salvia is changed each year.

Benches and water features are found throughout the garden at Three Timbers. The lush plantings are designed for multiseason bloom.

Camp Limber Lost

Upper St. Regis Lake was the site of many of the first Adirondack-style camps. In the early 1900s, a two-story cabin and outbuildings were constructed at Limber Lost. The original building has an unusual two-story screened porch with intricate twig railings. In 1989, Michael Bird of Adirondack Design drew plans for the rustic lakeside boathouse that is now the main residence. Bird's sister, Mary Beth, designed and installed the adjacent water gardens.

A large pond and waterfall were built with native stone, which is softened with sturdy perennials that blend naturally with the surrounding woods and lake. The pond's edge is planted with moisture-loving perennials such as globeflower *(Trollius chinensis* 'Golden Queen'*)*, marsh marigold *(Caltha palustris)*, bigleaf ligularia *(Ligularia dentata* 'Desdemona'*)*, and native ferns. The pond water is pumped from the lake and re-circulated through the rushing waterfall. Because of environmental concerns, only native aquatic plants are

The boathouse at Camp Limber Lost also serves as the main residence.

The borders of the water garden are planted with moisture-loving astilbe, groundsel, globeflower, and native ferns.

utilized. Sedges, spotted jewelweed *(Impatiens capensis)*, reeds, and water lilies have naturalized on their own.

A diverse selection of natives and hybrid perennials is artfully planted along the paths and shoreline. Low-maintenance sedum, daylilies, and astilbe planted along the flagstone paths stand up to the moderate foot traffic. Shade-loving ferns, hosta, and goatsbeard *(Aruncus)* are planted alongside the boathouse. In the main borders, daylilies, speedwell, foxglove, lupines, iris, and hardy rhododendrons have adapted to the lakeside setting. Stands of young white birch provide striking focal points. Bright red annual geraniums are generously utilized in window boxes and pots on the boathouse, docks, and guesthouses.

Above: Low-maintenance sedum, daylilies, and astilbe are planted along the flagstone paths.

Right: The boathouse residence provides a rustic backdrop for the water garden.

The original camp at Limber Lost, with the boathouse and water garden in the foreground

Stands of white birch provide striking focal points along the paths at Camp Limber Lost.

Plantings of hardy shrubs, perennials, and annuals soften the building foundations at Camp Rivermouth.

Camp Rivermouth

At Camp Rivermouth on Oseetah Lake, twenty years of horticultural experimentation has resulted in a garden of astonishing diversity. Native and hybridized plants are collected from around the Adirondack Park and grown in this USDA Zone 3 garden. More than a hundred species of woodland natives, roses, perennials, shrubs, grasses, and evergreens thrive throughout the picturesque waterfront setting. The extensive gardens flourish under the care of Junior "J.T." Thompson, who attended agricultural school in his native Jamaica and completed classes through Cornell University Cooperative Extension. The camp's owners keep a close hand in the garden during frequent weekend visits and extended stays in summer.

The lakefront Great Camp, near the village of Saranac Lake, was constructed between 1904 and 1914 and consists of the main house, guest cottages, and outbuildings. Plantings of hardy shrubs, perennials, and annuals soften the building foundations. The rustic log structures, painted brown and trimmed with red, blend with the wooded surroundings. Wide, deep porches, including a long screened veranda that faces the lake, are adorned with hanging baskets and hollowed-out log containers brimming with colorful annuals. The winding pathway down to the shoreline is flanked with stone walls spilling over with yellow native sedums (*Sedum spathulifolium*) in early summer. Later in the season, dragon's blood sedums (*Sedum spurium*) transform the stairway into a mass of brilliant scarlet red.

The main garden is nestled a quarter-mile uphill from the camp in a clearing carved from the redolent conifer forest. Giant, lichen-covered boulders protrude above a pancake-thin layer of barren soil. To bring life-

Asters, sedums, and ornamental kale add fall color to the driveway entrance garden.

giving sustenance to the site, loads of aged compost and manure were hauled in and mounded into raised beds one to two feet above the rock plateau. At the northwestern corner, a woodland border of natives and shade-loving perennials provides a gradual transition between the formal beds and adjacent cedar swamp. Adirondack-style cedar trellises, arbors, and benches scattered throughout the garden were built by Brent Rushlaw, the camp's former caretaker. A large, formal pergola brings visual scale to the transition between cultivated gardens and adjacent woods.

The beds are planted in warm and cool color schemes inspired by English garden writer Gertrude Jekyll. Old-fashioned English delphinium, hollyhocks, and foxgloves tower above drifts of astilbe, lady's mantle, and silvery lamb's ears *(Stachys byzantina)*. Strawberry foxglove *(Digitalis × mertonensis* 'Strawberry'*)* is a reliable, underused perennial with large rosy pink flowers and a long bloom time. Native wildflowers such as wild iris and marsh marigold *(Caltha palustris)* are collected from roadside ditches, marshes, and fields. Favorite varieties are sometimes given nicknames; a

towering cup plant *(Silphium perfoliatum)* found near the town of Jay is affectionately called "Jay's Giant."

In spring, tiny blooms of early snowdrops and crocus are followed by tulips, daffodils, and grape hyacinth *(Muscari)*, whose heady fragrance is unappealing to hungry deer. Forget-me-nots *(Myosotis)* and celandine poppy *(Stylophorum diphyllum)* are allowed to self-sow along a winding path to the camp, creating a river of

Above: A pathway to the lake is lined with hardy sedums.

Right: The limestone katydid sculpture is by West Virginia artist Lawrence Terrafranca.

Primroses and forget-me-nots (Myosotis) *blend companionably.*

blue and yellow. Around the main house, white and purple lenten rose *(Helleborus orientalis)* and bleeding heart *(Dicentra spectabilis)* bloom for several weeks.

Behind the arbor in the primary garden, Japanese primrose *(Primula japonica)* and drumstick primrose *(Primula denticulata)* are naturalized amid a sea of blue forget-me-nots. Yellow leopard's bane *(Doronicum)*, with its daisylike flowers, and cushion spurge *(Euphorbia polychroma)*, a long bloomer underused in Adirondack gardens, are planted near the foot of the arbor along a stone path. In the woodland garden,

cowslip *(Primula veris)* blooms in spring, summer, and again in fall, even in the snow.

Twenty varieties of own-root rugosa, shrub, climbing, Meidiland, and hybrid musk roses, including 'Dortmund', 'Grootendoorst', and 'Bonica', are selected for hardiness and disease resistance. Remarkably, several hybrid tea roses, including the single-flowered delicate pink 'Dainty Bess' and the heavily perfumed 'Bewitched', have performed well. Chemical pesticides are not used, though an occasional application of insecticidal soap controls mites and

A large pergola anchors the main garden at Camp Rivermouth.

Roses for the North Country

*R*oses are among the most beloved of all garden plants, but they are difficult to grow in the Adirondacks. Many hybrid varieties are grafted onto rootstock; in severe cold, they die back to the ground and the graft does not survive, although the often uninteresting rootstock may come back. The key to success is to choose own-root roses from the types listed here. A nursery professional can tell whether or not a rose is grafted. Heirloom Roses (listed in Resources) grows all plants on their own roots.

Buck: The more than seventy-five varieties developed by Dr. Griffith Buck at Iowa State University were bred for disease resistance, flower color, and winter hardiness (USDA Zone 4 without protection). They include 'Carefree Beauty', 'Prairie Sunset', and 'Distant Drums', a unique shade of bronze-brown and lavender.

Canadian Explorer: These roses are bred in Canada to withstand harsh winters (USDA Zones 3 and 4). All are shrubs, although 'William Baffin', one of the hardiest, can be trained as a climber. Most are red or pink; 'Henry Hudson' has fragrant white flowers

An ancient rambling rose of unknown origin at the Wikiosco estate, Lake George

and 'J.P. Connell' has pale yellow double blooms. 'John Davis' has old-fashioned blooms of candy pink with a golden center and is hardy to USDA Zone 2.

Meidiland: This ground-cover form is fast growing, disease resistant, and tolerant of poor growing conditions. Hardiness depends on the variety.

Native: *Rosa carolina, R. blanda,* and *R. virginiana* grow locally in the wild.

Floribunda: 'Nearly Wild' is one of the few floribundas that flourishes to USDA Zone 4.

Old-Fashioned: This group includes albas (USDA Zone 3); and gallicas, centifolias, polyanthas, wichurana ramblers, and damasks, all hardy to USDA Zone 4.

Rosa rubrifolia (syn. glauca): Exceptionally hardy, to USDA Zone 2, this rose is grown for its blue foliage tinged with purple. Insignificant pink flowers produce beautiful rust-red hips in late summer.

Rugosa: These roses are among the hardiest (USDA Zone 3) and are especially disease resistant and care-free. 'Hansa' has outstanding fragrance; 'Therese Bugnet' is exceptionally hardy, to USDA Zone 2.

Left: Roses at Camp Rivermouth are selected for hardiness and disease resistance.

Below: Forget-me-nots (Myosotis) *and celandine poppy* (Stylaphorum diphyllum) *are allowed to self-sow along a winding path, creating a river of blue and yellow.*

aphids. Japanese beetles are not a problem for the roses here as they are in many parts of the park. In fall, the hybrid tea roses and other select tender plants are lightly pruned and covered around the base with a foot of compost and soil to insulate against the winter cold. The larger shrub roses are wrapped in burlap.

Deer are regular visitors, so the main garden is surrounded by a five-foot-high electric fence. The vegetation around the camp buildings is sprayed with Deer-Off in early spring when plants begin leafing out and again every two months. In fall, rhododendrons, azaleas, and burning bush are enclosed with chicken wire to discourage deer from munching on tender new buds the following spring. ❧

*L*ake George, known as the "Queen of American Lakes," was first traversed by Native American tribes hundreds of years ago. The spring-fed lake with a backdrop of lush green mountains was the main waterway between the Hudson River and Lake Champlain. During the French and Indian Wars and the Revolutionary War, the region was a strategic stronghold, with Fort William Henry at the lake's south end and Fort Ticonderoga to the north.

In 1791, Thomas Jefferson journeyed with James Madison to New York State and Vermont. In a letter to his daughter Martha, Jefferson wrote: "Lake George is without comparison the most beautiful water I ever saw; formed by a contour of mountains into a basin thirty-five miles long, and from two to four miles broad, finely interspersed with islands, its waters limpid as crystal and the mountainsides covered with rich groves of thuja, silver fir, white pine, aspen and paper birch down to the water edge, here and there precipices of rock to checquer the scene and save it from monotony."

The Lost Gardens of Lake George

At the south end of the lake, the community of Caldwell, later named Lake George Village, was settled in 1810 by its founder, James Caldwell. Following the Civil War, Lake George became a summer playground for the wealthy and a hub for tourists traveling into the remote park by stagecoach, steamboat, and rail.

Many of the era's wealthy and famous, including artist Georgia O'Keeffe, photographer Alfred Stieglitz, *New York Times* publisher Adolph S. Ochs, and internationally acclaimed opera singer Marcella Sembrich, became summer residents. The road between Lake George Village and the town of Bolton Landing was known as Millionaire's Row for the proliferation of ex-travagant mansions that sprang up along Lake Shore Drive. Many socialites divided their time between the lake and nearby Saratoga Springs, renowned for its horse racing, social events, and curative mineral baths.

The grand estates on Millionaire's Row were an affirmation of social standing. The elaborate architecture was a conglomerate of various European styles. The accompanying gardens and landscaping were also of European taste, with precise, formal flower beds and expansive manicured lawns. Kathryn E. O'Brien's classic book *The Great and the Gracious on Millionaire's Row* makes numerous references to the elaborate landscaping of the estates on Lake George's western shore.

Large urns planted with annuals or tropicals were popular in the early 1900s and can still be found along the Bolton Road today.

A grand staircase at the Cramer villa on Millionaire's Row. Courtesy of Hugh Allen Wilson and Marshall Ford

The Gardens on Millionaire's Row

Erlowest

In the early 1900s, Edward Morse Shepard, a lawyer who made his fortune in railroad and mining holdings, built the Queen Anne–style mansion he named Erlowest. The granite house was classic in design, with a sweeping view of mountains and islands in the lake. Expansive lawns that sloped down to the water's edge were adorned with elaborate flower gardens and ornamental plantings. The natural beauty of the site was carefully preserved, and visitors strolled down deeply forested paths.

The mansion still stands and today is operated as an upscale inn and restaurant.

Albenia

George Foster Peabody, following the lead of his wealthy friends, purchased the former Colonel Price property on the southwestern shore of Lake George. The estate, consisting of a large Victorian home and several hundred acres of land, was named Albenia, Algonquin for "home of rest."

Peabody, born to modest means, had advanced through the ranks of the investment bank of Spencer Trask and Company to become a partner. Investment banks played an important role in the development of the United States in the latter part of the nineteenth century. There were vast business opportunities in

Erlowest. Courtesy of Hugh Allen Wilson and Marshall Ford.

Residence of E. M. Shepard, Lake George, N. Y.

coal and oil exploration, mining, farming, and public
utilities. Peabody focused his interests in the building
and financing of railroads. He became a local bene-
factor, donating his land holdings of Prospect Mountain and Hearthstone, both on the west side of Lake
George, for public use.

Peabody made sure that guests at Albenia had many
vantage points from which to enjoy the idyllic lake
view, even setting chairs on top of the roof. Brightly
colored geraniums were planted along the roof's edge.
A profusion of fresh flowers picked daily from the
gardens and greenhouse decorated the lavish rooms.

Peabody embellished the grounds, planting large
shade trees and ornamental shrubs, and building decorative stone walls and walkways, while maintaining
the natural, pristine setting. Guests enjoyed strolling
along the vast lawns and carefully tended flower gardens. In 1915, Albenia was sold to Peabody's friend
Adolph Ochs.

Bixby Estate

On Mohican Point, south of Bolton Landing, the
William K. Bixby family built an impressive Greek
Revival–style mansion. Finished in 1902, the house
was sited to take advantage of the breathtaking view
down the southern basin of the lake. A row of stately
elms with elegantly arching branches provided a
canopy of shade. Elaborate gardens with flowering
shrubs and perennials were tended by a bevy of gardeners. A picturesque walking bridge spanned the
outlet of a spring-fed pond. Much of the property was
preserved in its natural woodland state, with pathways
for leisurely walks in the woods. An informal wildflower meadow at the forest edge offered a naturalized
contrast to the neatly manicured grounds.

*Flower beds and lawn at
the William H. Bixby
estate. Courtesy of Bolton
Historical Museum.*

Villa Marie Antoinette

Dr. William Gerard Beckers, an immigrant from Germany who made a fortune by revolutionizing American dyemaking, bought ninety acres of land on Huddle Bay, between Bolton Landing and Diamond Point. Between 1916 and 1918, he built one of the most elaborate estates on Lake George, a compound of Spanish-style buildings named Villa Marie Antoinette after his wife. A stone wall, which cost $200,000 to build, enclosed acres of manicured lawns, lavish flower gardens, and ornate fountains and pools.

World War I brought shortages of many goods. Dyes for textiles and other manufacturing were formerly imported from Germany; American-made dyes, which replaced them, were inferior. Beckers brought German dyemaking technology to this country.

Villa Marie Antoinette became Beckers's year-round home, and he took an active interest in the community. He grew large quantities of fragrant white Oriental lilies, which were used at the annual high school graduation in Bolton Landing.

In the 1940s, the property changed hands several times and was opened as the Melody Manor, a restaurant and hotel. Maintenance costs and taxes became too steep and the mansion was torn down in 1953; its furnishings were auctioned. The gatehouse, which still stands, is as large and elegant as some of the lake's

Bixby's son William H. Bixby purchased the former Broesel home, just south of his father's estate. A grand double stairway made of cut stone led from the house to the expansive lawn below. Large urns were placed along the staircase, and small island beds dotted the lawn. Near the lake's shore, gently curving walking paths wound through a series of formal flower beds. The William K. Bixby home is one of the few remaining estates on Lake George still owned by the original family. Bixby's son's mansion also still stands and is privately owned.

Top: William H. Bixby estate. Courtesy of Bolton Historical Museum.

Left: The gardens at Villa Marie Antoinette, 1949. Richard K. Dean photo.

Left: Bayview

Below: Marcella Sembrich (far right) and her pupils at Bayview.

Both photographs courtesy of Marcella Sembrich Opera Museum.

other mansions themselves. The gatehouse was restored and is now an upscale antiques shop owned by Ginette and David Muslanka. Still remaining on the property are fountains with figures in the shape of lions, as well as pools, trellises, and a bridge from the original estate.

Bayview

On Bolton Bay, the William Demuth family built the mansion they named Bayview, which looked out onto an idyllic scene of peaceful waters interrupted by the occasional small island. The grounds were embellished with woodland walking paths, gently curving driveways, and ornamental flower beds. Meandering pathways led from the house along the water's edge. One quiet inlet there is named Hydrangea Bay for the long row of hydrangea bushes still in evidence along the shore.

Photographs show a grand flower border along the stone terracing in front of the house. The walkway that led to the shore was lined with colorful annuals. Shrubs planted around the house and on the lawn were neatly clipped into curved shapes. Rustic benches and large classic urns filled with tropicals and annuals were scattered about the grounds. The veranda was softened with vines that covered the railing and extended to the second story.

Bayview was later the part-time residence of internationally acclaimed opera singer Marcella Sembrich. After a distinguished career with the Metropolitan Opera that took her around the world, Sembrich occupied a small studio on the property where she taught her voice pupils. Now a museum, the studio is set in a tall stand of pines along the shore. The nearby woodland pathways are planted with old specimens of rhododendrons and azaleas. Sembrich enjoyed puttering around the gardens in her later years, and her gardening hand tools are in the museum collection. The museum is undergoing modern updates, including restoration of the grounds.

Looking onto Bolton Bay from Bayview. Courtesy of Hugh Allen Wilson and Marshall Ford.

Villa Nirvana

Green Island, in Bolton Landing, is best known for its world-class resort, The Sagamore. Many of the investors in the original hotel had summer homes adjacent to the hotel grounds. John Boulton Simpson built Villa Nirvana, a Victorian-style mansion and spectacular showplace, with every part of the grounds beautifully landscaped.

Head gardener Ranny Wilson was a consummate plantsman, having memorized the botanical names of each plant on the grounds and in the conservatories. Flower beds were meticulously groomed and trees neatly pruned. Shrub topiaries were trained in shapes resembling creatures of nature: a starfish, butterfly, and tortoise. A stand of peonies spelled the words "Villa Nirvana." (A popular feature in gardens of the time was to have the name of the estate displayed with beds of flowers.) A rustic playhouse had log porch supports, twig railings, and a sunburst design at the peak of the roof.

Plantings flank the broad verandah at Villa Nirvana. J. A. Thatcher photo, courtesy of Hugh Allen Wilson and Marshall Ford.

Right: Mrs. John Boulton Simpson in the gardens at Villa Nirvana. J. A. Thatcher photo, courtesy of Hugh Allen Wilson and Marshall Ford.

Below: The greenhouse and arbor at present-day Nirvana Farm.

Nirvana Farm, directly across from Villa Nirvana on the mainland, supplied the estate with eggs, milk, and fresh produce. Two Victorian-style glass greenhouses, heated by steam pipes, held annual and vegetable seedlings in spring. The spectacular specimens of tropicals and cactus that adorned the grounds were stored in the greenhouses during the winter.

During the Gilded Age, a favorite challenge for gardening enthusiasts was coaxing their night-blooming cereus *(Epiphyllum oxypetalum)* to flower. Each fragrant creamy white bloom of this cactus, native to Central and South America, lasts just one night. This extraordinary event was great cause for an impromptu all-night party. At Villa Nirvana, an exceptional

specimen of night-blooming cereus was said to have bloomed thirty or forty times in one summer.

Today, Nirvana still stands, although the facade of the house has been altered and the gardens are no longer in evidence. Nirvana Farm is now a privately owned estate, with remnants of the gardens still in existence, including a large vine-covered arbor and one of the greenhouses. Two long borders of daylilies, daisies, and goldenrod run from the house to the lakeshore.

stairs, terracing, pools, benches, and patios that composed the structure of the formal garden. Winding staircases led visitors from the house to the horticultural Eden below.

The garden was laid out in formal symmetrical beds, with wide expanses of lawn in between and a large, rectangular pool at the center. Thousands of gold- and silver-colored fish swam in the waters, their jewel-like forms glistening in the sun. Water, in both natural and

The gardens at the Knapp Estate on Shelving Rock. Jesse Wooley photo.

The Knapp Estate

One of the most elaborate area gardens was at Shelving Rock, on the east side of Lake George. In 1885, George O. Knapp, president of Union Carbide, bought 7700 acres of land, including ten miles of shoreline. There he built a grand mansion on a ledge carved out of the side of a steep mountain several hundred feet above the lake. A cable car ferried visitors from the lakeshore boathouse up the precarious slope directly into the mansion through an archway in the basement.

Just below the massive retaining walls of the house, a large Italian-style ornamental garden was completed in 1902 at the cost of $40,000 (more than $830,000 in 2004 dollars). An enormous kitchen garden of fruits and vegetables supplied the kitchen with food. Granite quarried from the property was used to build the walls,

man-made features, was a recurring theme. A spring-fed waterfall tumbled down the mountainside into a brook that ran through the center of the garden. A large gazebo adorned with starburst-patterned twigwork was perched on a rock above nearby Shelving Rock Falls. Other gazebos, benches, and arbors made of twigs and logs were scattered throughout the grounds.

The grand flower borders that lined the grass promenade were outlined in precisely cut stone. Native cedar, birch, and conifers lent a natural backdrop with an understory of ferns and moss. A large rose garden was laid out in precise squares with tanbark walks in between. It was said that the garden contained nearly every variety of rose that would grow in this harsh climate. A massive colonnade to one side was supported by a row of Roman-style pillars. The ground beneath the pergola was covered with square stone tiles, and a lattice roof supported an array of vigorous vines. Large stone urns were filled with colorful flowers; a sundial and other statuary provided decorative focal points.

The elaborate Knapp mansion burned to the ground in 1917 and was never rebuilt. The gardens are said to have lasted into the 1930s, when they were no longer kept up and succumbed to the elements of nature.

George O. Knapp died shortly after World War II at the age of ninety-two. His heirs sold all but thirty-five acres of the property to the state of New York, and the land is now preserved as a state park, open to visitors for hiking and exploring. The Knapp family still retains a home on the lake shore.

Other Gardens on Lake George

Kathryn E. O'Brien's book makes brief reference to other gardens on Millionaire's Row. At Green Harbour, Harold Pitcairn's secluded retreat, exotic orchids were kept in a glass greenhouse.

Trinity Rock, railroad magnate George Cramer's villa, was first mentioned in 1873 in Seneca Ray Stoddard's *Guidebook for Lake George*. O'Brien's book says the estate was known for its beautifully kept grounds, which were tended by twenty-two gardeners.

An antique postcard shows profusely blooming plants, probably hydrangeas, along the front of the mansion. Another view along the side of the house (see page 51) shows a grand staircase flanked with lush flower borders and ornamental trees. Massive stone planters were placed at the top and bottom of the stairs.

Recluse Island was the summer home of Dr. Pliny T. Sexton, a member of the U.S. Supreme Court during the late 1800s. Stoddard described the setting: "[An] encircling belt of whitened stones, rustic vases and arbors, cozy seats, swinging hammocks, and pleasant flower-skirted walks, winding about among the trees with many gay banners floating over it, make the little island-home beautiful as a dream of fairyland."

In the Great Depression of the 1930s, fortunes were lost and many of the mansions on Millionaire's Row changed hands. Some of the mansions fell into disrepair; some were torn down to make way for the rental cottages and motels that now occupy much of the lakeshore. In the past twenty years, land values have sharply increased. Some of the remaining mansions are being restored as private residences, exclusive resorts, and fine dining establishments. ❧

Le Grand Cramer Residence, Lake George, N. Y.

Hydrangea bushes flank the Cramer estate in this postcard view. Courtesy of Hugh Allen Wilson and Marshall Ford.

Lake George Gardens of Today

Wikiosco, "Home of Beautiful Waters"

Fortunately, not all of the mansions on Millionaire's Row were lost. George Peabody's brother Royal Canfield Peabody built a magnificent English Tudor–style mansion that he named Wikiosco, meaning "home of beautiful waters." The house was built to last for many generations and is one of the finest remaining examples of luxury and elegance that exemplified Millionaire's Row. The property changed hands several times during the twentieth century; it was most notably owned by local entrepreneur and philanthropist Charles R. Wood. The structure was operated as the summer resort Holiday House and a restaurant, Blenheim-on-the-Lake, before being returned to a private residence. Dr. Stephen Serlin and his wife, Kate,

bought the property in 1990 and restored the house and grounds to their original splendor.

The gardens that undoubtedly graced the original estate probably included an old rambling rose that still clambers over a large boulder at the center of the front lawn. The rose, of unknown heritage, is the centerpiece of the present gardens. A rock wall extending past the boulder is a backdrop for ferns, astilbe,

Above: Exposed ledge flanks the gardens at the Wikiosco mansion.

Right: Wikiosco enjoys commanding views of Lake George.

daylilies, purple loosestrife, and bee balm. A classic four-tiered fountain sits in a tranquil reflecting pool. Vining ivy and Virginia creeper soften the imposing stone facade of the house. A large climbing rose flourishes at the bottom of a grand staircase, which is adorned with stone urns filled with yellow marigolds, red geraniums, and spiky dracaena. A magnificent specimen of Japanese maple *(Acer palmatum)*, which is difficult to grow this far north, adds deep burgundy foliage to the lush mix of color and texture.

Quiet Elegance at Allenhurst

Many older homes on Lake George have been in the same family for several generations. Hugh Allen Wilson's family came to the region after the Revolutionary War and later moved to a small lakeside house in Bolton Landing. The original cottage at Allenhurst was built in 1887 and was soon enlarged into a grand two-story Queen Anne–style wood-frame home with an expansive veranda and unusual second-story balcony. The rolling emerald green lawn stretching 150 feet to the lakeshore is reminiscent of the grand oceanfront estates in Newport, Rhode Island.

Wilson's first attempts at gardening were shortly after World War II when he began raising roses. A Queen of Denmark rose handed down from his great-grandmother is thought to be 150 years old. Hardy to USDA Zone 4, the sweetly fragrant rose is extremely disease resistant and roots easily from cuttings. Wilson found that most roses were too temperamental, however, so he began growing hardy perennials and

The grand front steps at Wikiosco are decorated with flower-filled urns, a favorite garden ornament in the early twentieth century.

shrubs. Along the side of the house, a diverse selection of evergreens and deciduous trees and shrubs includes old rhododendrons and a large specimen of purple-leaved Japanese maple. The back garden is a rich tapestry of perennials and old-fashioned shrubs, including a magnificent specimen of beautybush *(Kolkwitzia amabilis)* dating to the 1920s. Partially shaded by a canopy of stately trees, the rear garden is planted with reliable perennials including bee balm,

daylilies, hosta, iris, balloon flower, phlox, tickseed, and delphinium. Snow-on-the-mountain *(Euphorbia marginata)*, with its dramatic white-and-green foliage, complements more traditional annuals—marigolds, cleome, and nicotiana—providing summer-long color. A vigorous trumpet vine *(Campsis radicans)* is trained on a sturdy metal arbor over the garage door.

Caretaker Marshall Ford has assisted Wilson with the gardens for more than twenty years. A large,

Above: An impressive specimen of beautybush at Allenhurst dates to the 1920s.

Left: The shore garden

circular bed of ostrich fern and hostas in front of the
house was the first of several plantings he installed.
The ferns, popular during Victorian times, were rescued from a nearby abandoned garden, and the hostas
were dug from an old local farmstead. In 2002, Ford
built a stone wall on the shore next to the boat dock,
where he planted small conifers and an assortment
of annuals and perennials.

In keeping with the traditional theme, antique and
reproduction urns decorate the grounds by the house,
on the expansive lawn, at the dock, and along the
water's edge. Painted in classic colors of white and
deep green, the urns are planted with silver-foliaged
wormwood *(Artemisia)*, coleus in sizzling hues, and
Chinese spinach *(Amaranthus tricolor)*. Wave Hybrids
petunias, million bells *(Calibrachoa)*, licorice plant
(Helichrysum petiolare), verbena, and nasturtiums spill
over the sides like cascading necklaces.

*A lawn with an island bed of hostas and
ostrich ferns (above) and flower-filled
urns (right) at Allenhurst hark back to
more formal times.*

Left: Cottage-style perennial borders flank a garden shed at Allenhurst.

Below: The border alongside the Forman house is an eclectic mix of shrubs, dwarf conifers, and reliable perennials.

A Garden of Diversity

Dave Forman's property near Bolton Landing is a fine illustration of the surprising diversity of plants that can be grown in the harsh climate of the Adirondacks. The one-acre garden boasts nearly six hundred varieties, mainly herbaceous perennials.

Originally from Troy, Forman lived and gardened in Florida and New Jersey before moving to the Adirondacks in the mid-1990s. In 1997, he installed his first garden, a collection of dwarf conifers, adjacent to his impressive log home. Flanking the conifers, a mix of heaths and heathers perform well in the well drained, sandy soil. The varied shapes, colors, and textures offer year-round interest.

Forman soon added more raised beds on top of the naturally rocky soil, amending them with topsoil, peat, and Garden-Tone 4-6-6, a complete organic fertilizer. He enriched the large vegetable plot behind

Heaths and heathers, adjacent to Dave Forman's dwarf conifers, are protected in winter by deep snow cover.

the house with compost. The surrounding forest is mainly coniferous, so leaf mulch is at a premium.

Forman's other plant collections are equally impressive. There are more than fifty German iris cultivars and twenty additional varieties of iris. Nearly fifty cultivars of daylilies are scattered throughout most of the beds. Bulbous lilies are well represented, with thirty different types. Siberian pea-tree (*Caragana arborescens* 'Pendula') is exceptionally hardy and underutilized in

North Country gardens. The weeping deciduous shrub has shiny green leaves and clusters of pealike pale yellow flowers that appear in late spring.

Growing vines is a challenge in the Adirondacks, where long, cold freezes can kill plants back to the ground. Forman grows several hardy clematis, including 'Comtesse de Bouchard', 'Duchess of Albany', 'Royalty', and 'Shooun'. He lets a large patch of violas self-sow in a "river of pansies." Campanulas, a staple

Thirty different types of bulbous lilies, including pink and yellow 'Kiss Me Kate', are well represented in Forman's garden.

in many Adirondack gardens, are well represented here. One notable variety is 'Cherry Bells' *(Campanula punctata)*, a long-blooming cultivar with large, bell-shaped pink flowers. Roses are selected for hardiness and disease resistance; varieties include rugosas and Meidiland types such as 'Meipelta'.

Because of the moderating effect of Lake George and the consistent winter snow cover, Forman successfully grows many plants that are normally hardy only to USDA Zone 6. Bluebeard *(Caryopteris × clandonensis* 'Longwood Blue'), a deciduous shrub with silvery foliage, has violet-blue flowers that appear in late summer. Foxtail lily *(Eremurus × isabellinus* 'Shelford Hybrids'), with long, spiky flowers of yellow, orange, or cream, has done exceptionally well. Bear's foot hellebore *(Helleborus foetidus)* has leaves shaped like a bear's claw and chartreuse-green blooms in early spring.

Hostas, groundsel, goatsbeard (Aruncus), *and astilbe in Forman's shade garden make a tapestry of flower and foliage color.*

Loblolly

The northern portion of Lake George is vastly different from the more heavily populated south. From Bolton Landing to Hague, a distance of fifteen miles, the lake is largely undeveloped. Route 9N slithers precariously around the back side of Tongue Mountain (one of only two rattlesnake habitats in the Adirondacks), hugging the shoreline through Sabbath Day Point and Silver Bay before arriving at the quaint village of Hague.

Near the center of town is the secluded waterfront garden at Loblolly (named for a type of southern pine). The single-level home with large picture windows showcases uninterrupted views of Anthony's Nose to the north and the unspoiled shoreline of the lake's east side.

The gardens at Loblolly began as an informal planting of wildflowers. When the look eventually became too unkempt, the owner, who lives there summers, hired landscapers David and JoAnne DeFranco to replace the free-flowing meadows with cultivated flower beds. The annual wildflowers were replaced with easy-to-maintain perennials such as coral bells, purple coneflower, black-eyed Susan, tickseed, sedums, speedwell, and mallow.

The lower property near the house was once a streambed, and the clay soil is naturally soggy. The DeFrancos built raised beds for better drainage and hauled in compost and leaf mulch to improve the soil. Moisture-loving plants thrive here, including ligularia, astilbe, bugbane *(Actaea simplex)*, hosta,

Loblolly's seating area offers spectacular views across Lake George.

gooseneck loosestrife *(Lysimachia clethroides)*, and dwarf arctic willow *(Salix purpurea* 'Nana').

The garden is designed for peak bloom during July and August, when the house is most visited. Perennials are selected for hardiness, long bloom time, and foliage interest. Quick-growing annuals such as snapdragon, baby's breath *(Gypsophila)*, Wave Hybrids petunias, alyssum, and dahlias fill in gaps. Oriental lilies, a favorite of the owner, perfume the air with their heavenly scent in August. Sturdy shrubs including cinquefoil, creeping barberry, and spirea give the garden structure. A cedar Adirondack-style bench, built by Eugene Slade, provides a focal point in the main garden.

Deer are a frequent problem, so the DeFrancos use Deer-Off and mothballs during the growing season and cover the shrubs with netting in winter to discourage hungry foragers. Woodchucks, moles, and voles are also a nuisance, for which various organic pest controls are used.

The entry garden (left) and island perennial beds (below) brim with color.

Lakeside Cottage Gardens

The east side of the lake, which includes the peninsulas of Assembly Point and Cleverdale, has fewer improved roads than the flatter, more exposed west side, so development was largely limited to modest summer camps on small lots. Many cottages are built on steep banks, with the accompanying challenges to gardening.

Assembly Point is a long, narrow finger packed tightly with quaint, older camps, many of them unweatherized. At the year-round home of Myron and Barbara Rappaport, an exceptionally steep, wooded slope between the house and lake presented difficult landscaping challenges. Designer David Campbell tucked fertile pockets of soil between boulders and planted ground covers and sturdy shrubs such as cinquefoil, rhododendrons, and conifers. He added low-maintenance perennials—hosta, daylilies, cranesbill geraniums, and black-eyed Susans—for multi-season color. The largely green tapestry has many

Above: Lemon yellow tickseed (Coreopsis verticillata) *'Moonbeam' (foreground) is one of many long-blooming perennials grown at Loblolly.*

Below: A slate-paved landing midway down the slope of the Rappaport garden offers a secluded place for conversation.

An attractive flagstone wall forms the foundation of the Cleverdale garden of Bob and Betsy Birchenough.

subtle variations: deep forest green, midrange olive, and silvery blue-green.

The large boulders along the winding flagstone path suggest a native mountainside, their craggy edges softened by the surrounding plants. A grouping of bright red Adirondack chairs on a slate landing midway down the slope gives visitors a secluded place to relax. Myron enjoys working with metal and built the many whimsical sculptures around the property. Several simple cut-out figures above the boathouse suggest a family waving at passing boats. Handrails and gates are also personalized with metal decorations.

Just up the lake, Bob and Betsy Birchenough's home in Cleverdale exemplifies a typical lakefront cottage. Raised beds along the front of the house are filled with late-summer bloomers such as gayfeather, purple coneflower, asters, sedums, and phlox. The stone wall retains heat in early spring, warming the soil. Later in the season, shade trees keep the bed from getting too hot. A tidy border along the side of the yard is an attractive foreground to the view of the lake. Visitors can take refuge from mosquitoes on a comfortable screened porch that looks over the gardens and lake. ❧

The steep slope of the Rappaport garden presents extra challenges to the gardener.

Backdrops and Garden Adornments

*A*s in Japan, where the surrounding views, or shakkei, are mindfully incorporated into a garden's design, many of today's Adirondack gardens are situated to take advantage of the beautiful scenery. That natural backdrop lends itself to informal design; cottage-style borders are much more in place here than clipped, formal beds. Many gardeners incorporate native plants into their designs, seeing their plots as an extension of wild habitat. Near the hamlet of Indian Lake, for example, Pieter and Arlene Kien allow native milkweed, which is a host plant for monarch butterfly larvae, to naturalize among their hybrid cultivars.

The Great Camp era, from the 1870s to 1930s, heralded the beginning of rustic-style architecture, which has enjoyed a resurgence in popularity in recent years. Natural materials such as wood, stone, and twigs, as well as metal, were used to construct camps, furniture, and crafts. The distinct style spread across the United States and today is particularly used in the Rocky Mountain region. Many of the rustic chairs, benches, and tables found in

today's Adirondack camps and cottages are created by local artisans. Not surprisingly, classic Adirondack-style chairs are always a popular choice.

Spectacular stands of white birch are found throughout the region. Native Americans used the waterproof bark to make canoes, wigwams, and baskets. Today, birch bark embellishes mirrors, boxes, and other household adornments. Local gardeners also use the bark to decorate their gardens to great effect. Log or twig arbors, trellises, and fences are used frequently, too. Some are mainly ornamental; others support plants, create a barrier, or offer shade from hot afternoon sun.

Top: In Warrensburg, Teresa Whalen decorates her rustic garden shed with birch bark window boxes.

Right: Ruth Prime's perennial border near Lake Placid is designed to take advantage of a spectacular view of Whiteface Mountain.

Above: At Camp Rivermouth, a lone rustic bench provides a focal point.

Below: The rustic-style gazebo at Camp Woodmere is actually a pump house for the camp's water supply.

Trellises, arbors, and planters made of logs, twigs, and branches incorporate elements of surrounding forest into the gardens of Pam Doré (top), Camp Rivermouth (middle) and Cheley Witte (below).

An old wooden wheel-barrow (below) is still useful in TeresaWhalen's garden.

At Camp Owaissa, a bright burst of flowers leads the eye to the magnificent backdrop.

A rustic twig fence flanks Charlie Atwood-King and Karen Lamitie-King's garden.

In the garden of Charlie Atwood-King and Karen Lamitie-King, near Malone, chairs are placed near the banks of the brook that runs along their property.

Adirondack gardeners mix ingenuity with a sense of whimsy. Kathy Sweeney of Crystal Lake planted flowers in an old canoe that was beyond repair.

An elaborate twig arbor at the entrance to the Charlie Atwood-King and Karen Lamitie-King garden.

ublic gardens in the Adirondack region are few and far between, most likely because of the amount of effort required in such a short growing season. What public gardens lack in sheer number, however, they more than make up for in quality. Each of the three major public gardens within the Blue Line—the gardens at the Adirondack Museum in the middle of the Adirondack Park, the Colonial Garden in Elizabethtown, and the King's Garden at Fort Ticonderoga, at the northern extremity of Lake George—has evolved along its own unique path, exhibiting vastly different styles and characteristics.

Public Plantings

The Adirondack Museum Gardens

One of the greatest treasures of the North Country is the Adirondack Museum in Blue Mountain Lake. Opened in 1957, the museum chronicles the history of the region from the mid-1800s to the present with twenty major outdoor and indoor exhibits. Antique boats, original twig furniture, camp buildings, and environmental illustrations paint a picture of what life was like in the park during the past 150 years.

The region was first settled by Miles Tyler Merwin in 1867. He built a cabin and barn on the site where the museum now stands, later adding guest cabins and a small hotel. Despite the short season and the difficulties of the site, summer visitors cleared the woods, dug roots and rocks from the soil, hauled in topsoil to create gardens, and filled them with flowers, herbs, and vegetables. In the area now known as Merwin Hill, plants descended from these early gardens can still be found: hosta, daylilies, periwinkle (*Vinca* spp.), and even Oregon grape *(Mahonia aquifolium)*, which is not normally hardy this far north.

The museum gardens were first cultivated by Mary Hochschild, wife of founder Harold K. Hochschild. The grounds are a living exhibit of mature trees, shrubs, and perennials, many indigenous. Mary Hochschild grew up in New Jersey and spent her summers in Keene Valley, where she first experienced the challenges of gardening in the Adirondacks.

Flower boxes along the Adirondack Museum's visitors' deck are planted with colorful annuals.

Left: Woodland garden adjacent to the Adirondack Museum's Road and Rail Building

Below: Perennial border at the center of the museum complex

The museum is perched on a hillside 220 feet above Blue Mountain Lake; at 2,000 feet in elevation, it lies in USDA Zone 3. The terrain is rugged and inhospitable, consisting of a thin, barren layer of soil atop solid bedrock. Hochschild had truckloads of topsoil hauled in to build beds two feet deep for perennials and six feet deep for trees and shrubs.

Near the center of the museum complex, a spectacular perennial border is framed by a wood rail fence. The garden contains a diverse collection of perennials: Asiatic lilies, cranesbill geraniums, beard-tongue *(Penstemon barbatus)*, globe thistle *(Echinops)*, spiderwort, iris, daylilies, bleeding heart, tickseed, phlox, gayfeather, bee balm, purple coneflower, and goldenrod.

A stone wall along the south side of the Road and Rail Building serves as a backdrop to a colorful woodland garden. Foliage plants, including hosta, fern, coral bells, and spotted dead nettle *(Lamium maculatum* 'White Nancy'), are complemented by flowering astilbe, cranesbill geraniums, iris, and monkshood. Virginia creeper softens the wall and also grows up the sides of many of the buildings; it turns a brilliant scarlet red in fall. Because hostas, a staple of the museum gardens, are a favorite of deer, egg sulfur spray is applied every few weeks to deter these hungry marauders. Home remedies to discourage deer are many and varied. A basic egg sulfur spray consists of one

Sunset Cottage, a fine example of mosaic twig work, is the backdrop for plantings of sturdy shrubs such as spirea and barberry.

slightly beaten egg mixed with one quart water and applied to affected plants with a sprayer. Other variations include garlic and capsaicin, source of the intense flavor in hot peppers.

At the southwest corner of the Road and Rail Building, a visitors' deck looks out onto the lake. Brightly colored annuals fill long window boxes stretching the entire length of the L-shaped balcony. Marigolds, petunias, pansies, begonias, and speedwell provide a spectacular foreground to the breathtaking view of Blue Mountain Lake.

Shrubs are difficult to grow in the North Country, but the museum uses them to great effect. Shrubby cinquefoil is the longest blooming of all the plants at the museum. From June into September, this sturdy bush produces yellow or white flowers that look like the blooms on strawberry plants. In June and July, the intense perfume of a fifty-year-old mockorange *(Philadelphus coronarius)* fills the air around the Road and Rail Building. Peegee hydrangea *(Hydrangea paniculata* 'Grandiflora') and hills-of-snow hydrangea *(H. arborescens)* bloom in late summer and early fall, providing color at a time when many other plants have finished flowering.

Rhododendrons and azaleas are also scarce this far north, but Exbury azaleas *(Rhododendron* 'Exbury Hybrids') from the original gardens continue to flourish. On Merwin Hill, many native shrubs thrive in the

wooded forest. Several viburnums, including arrowwood *(Viburnum dentatum)*, hobble-bush *(V. lantanoides)*, and American cranberrybush viburnum *(V. trilobum)* produce white flowers in June and small, shiny berries in August.

When the museum was built, many existing trees were preserved and incorporated into the landscape. Impressive stands of sugar maple, which turn brilliant orange in fall, date to the days of Merwin. Near the Logging Building are groves of trees most often timbered in the heyday of logging: spruce, hemlock, white pine, and balsam fir. Northern white cedar and larch complement stands of white birch and quaking balsam poplars.

The hillside where Merwin and his group of summer residents once lived was renovated in the 1980s. Invasive nonnative plants—escapees from old gardens of the summer inhabitants—were weeded out, and natives and wildflowers were encouraged to repopulate the woods. The hillside is now alive with spring favorites, including purple trillium *(Trillium erectum)*; jack-in-the-pulpit *(Arisaema triphyllum)*; Indian poke *(Veratrum viride)*; blue bead lily *(Clintonia borealis)*; and the endearing pink lady's slipper *(Cypripedium acaule)*.

Several plants in the museum garden self-sow each year, including common foxglove *(Digitalis purpurea)*, yellow foxglove *(D. grandiflora)*, sweet William, and mullein. A garden at the front of the Mark W. Potter Education Center is planted with bee balm, purple coneflower, phlox, meadow sage *(Salvia pratensis)*, yarrow, and asters, all of which attract butterflies.

Besides Mary Hochschild, others have been instrumental in developing and maintaining the grounds. Jim Cooney was the head gardener of the museum grounds for many years. Now retired, he is well known for his passion for gardening and his years of expertise. The Gardens and Grounds group, a volunteer organization at the museum, assists with the maintenance of the museum gardens and participates in educational programs that address regional gardening techniques and concerns.

Astilbes and daylilies frame a view of the Marion River Carry building at the Adirondack Museum.

The Colonial Garden

In 1954, the Essex County Historical Society was formed in the hamlet of Elizabethtown. The following year, the school district voted to give a two-story brick schoolhouse at the center of town for use as a museum. Dr. and Mrs. Ira Younker, avid amateur gardeners and summer residents of the nearby town of Lewis, were asked if they had any ideas to improve the grounds. The Younkers proposed constructing a garden modeled after the significant horticultural masterpieces of Colonial America: Mount Vernon, Monticello, and Williamsburg. The gardens at Hampton Court in England provided further inspiration.

With the guidance of Lake Placid landscape architect Frank Politi, Williamsburg landscape architect Alden Hopkins, and a horticultural expert from Cornell University, the master plan of the garden was conceived. The ambitious project was completed and opened to the public in July 1956, and is maintained

Colonial Garden, ca. 1956. Courtesy of Adirondack History Center.

by volunteers from the Essex County Adirondack Garden Club.

Elements of Colonial-era landscape design are clearly evident. A lush, grassy lawn area is surrounded by neatly symmetrical flower borders. Wide gravel pathways edged with brick follow the perimeter. The central axis bed is planted with herbs, annuals, and perennials. A major focal point is the summerhouse, a large gazebo in eighteenth-century style with comfortable benches where visitors can enjoy the shade. Directly across from the summerhouse is a 1776 embossed-lead cistern with a dolphin spout that was brought from Barn Hall in Ewhurst, England.

The elegant, white, classical-style fence that graces the entrance was inspired by one found at Thomas Jefferson's home, Monticello. Plantings at the front include North Country staples such as hosta and daylilies. Just inside the entrance is a stone inscribed with "And the Glory of the Garden / It shall never pass away." The walls and gates at the back of the garden are replicas of those found at the Capitol in Williamsburg. An eighteenth-century sundial made of Portland stone was brought to the United States from Kirby Mallory Hall near Leicester, England. The brick pattern that surrounds the sundial is copied from the rotunda at the University of Virginia. Iron benches

Below: Colonial Garden's center bed and gazebo and the antique cistern

Facing page: A reproduction of a Mount Vernon iron bench in the Colonial Garden

placed along the rear brick walls are replicas of those found at Mount Vernon and were reproduced by the Williamsburg ironmongers.

The garden is enclosed by a hedge of cedar and softened with a variety of sturdy trees and shrubs. White birch is planted in the corners, and hemlock is placed at the front and back. Lilac, crab apple, and hawthorn are underplanted with viburnum, flowering quince, spirea, and ninebark *(Physocarpus opulifolius)*.

The original design, which emphasized annual and perennial flower varieties grown during Colonial times, has been amended to include sturdier modern hybrids. Annual snapdragons, calliopsis *(Coreopsis tinctoria)*, speedwell, red salvia, melampodium, heliotrope, and begonias are interspersed among reliable perennials, including bee balm, hostas, daylilies, tickseed, and astilbe.

The King's Garden

Strategically located atop a jutting peninsula between Lake George and Lake Champlain, Fort Ticonderoga was originally a French stronghold known as Fort Carillon, but for centuries before any European outpost overlooked the Champlain Valley, this region had been cultivated by Native Americans. Found artifacts suggest that indigenous tribes grew crops at this location as long as four thousand years ago, making this one of the oldest continuously cultivated sites in North America.

In the eighteenth century, crucial battles were fought over the lands nestled between the foothills of the Adirondacks and the Green Mountains of Vermont. During the French and Indian Wars, the loamy soil provided the soldiers at Fort Carillon a full complement of food crops, grown in precisely laid-out

plots: lettuce, carrots, cabbage, beans, onions, leeks, cucumbers, and herbs.

Fort Carillon was captured by the British, who renamed it Ticonderoga, meaning "land between the waters." During the Revolutionary War, a six-acre garden fed the hungry garrison troops. After the British were ousted from the fort in 1777, it fell into disrepair and the gardens succumbed to weeds and brush.

In 1820, William Ferris Pell, a successful business owner from New York City, bought the fort and 546 acres of surrounding land with dreams of restoring the now-plundered ruins. He built The Pavilion, a Federal-style inn, to accommodate tourists. An avid horticulturist, Pell planted the grounds with herbs, fruits imported from Europe, and numerous varieties of trees, including Lombardy poplar, black locust, catalpa, magnolia, and horse chestnut.

In the early 1900s, The Pavilion was converted into a summer residence. The grounds were improved with new outbuildings, fruit orchards, and a large kitchen garden. In 1912, Pell's grandson Stephen and his wife, Sarah, enclosed the one-acre ornamental gardens with

a nine-foot-tall brick wall. They named it Le Jardin du Roi, or "The King's Garden," the name found on French and British maps. The antique-style wall, with rough stones placed at random into the masonry, enclosed a long rectangle stretching from the main house. Symmetrical beds and formal paths were surrounded by lush green lawn. The Colonial Revival–style garden was filled with an impressive array of trees, shrubs, vines, and perennials. A circular pond in the center of the lawn served as the main focal point.

In 1920, the Pells hired Marian Cruger Coffin, one of the first women landscape architects in the United States, to create a more formal and fashionable garden within the existing walls. Coffin is best known for designing the famed gardens of the DuPont family's Winterthur estate in Delaware.

Coffin's design included four separate planting quadrants, each containing four smaller beds. Neatly clipped barberry hedges lined the herringbone-patterned brick pathways. Coffin utilized carefully orchestrated color themes, from cool pastel shades of globe thistle *(Echinops)* and sage *(Salvia azurea)* near

The King's Garden as seen from the air, ca. 1940. Fort Ticonderoga Museum collection.

The Pavilion, transitioning to the hot colors of zinnias, calliopsis *(Coreopsis tinctoria)*, and marigolds at the opposite end. The round water lily pond was replaced with a rectangular reflecting pool with cutaway corners. In 1937, noted sculptor and Pell cousin Anna Hyatt Huntington created the statue *The Young Diana* that still graces the center of the pool.

The enclosed wall creates its own microclimate, offering protection from harsh winter winds off the lake. The brick walls and pathways absorb and retain heat, warming the soil so plants get a head start in early spring. Several saucer magnolias *(Magnolia × soulangiana)*, which aren't normally found this far north, still survive from the original garden.

At the opposite corner from The Pavilion is a two-story brick teahouse. Chippendale benches, potted plants, and imported statuary create strategic focal points, leading the eye through the garden. A shaded alcove with a cozy seating area offers respite from hot summer sun. Small windows shaped like gun ports reveal glimpses of the pastoral landscape beyond. A wrought-iron gate perfectly frames a view of the European-style allée of poplars leading toward the fort.

During the next several decades, the gardens underwent many changes. Coffin's vivid color scheme shifted to more traditional English-style pastel colors. The Pell family hosted family events and occasionally opened the gardens to the public until John H. G. Pell's death in 1987; then the garden slowly succumbed to neglect. The board of trustees at Fort Ticonderoga voted to include the gardens and Pavilion as part of the museum's resources.

Facing page: Zinnias and tiger lilies frame the view toward the reflecting pool and The Pavilion.

Antique touches include the wrought-iron gate (right) and decorative urns atop the wall (below).

Left: An unusual two-story brick teahouse stands at one corner of the King's Garden.

Below: The Young Diana has stood in the garden since 1937.

The Garden Conservancy recognized the site as "a masterwork American garden" in 1992 and was enlisted to help in the garden's restoration and preservation. With the support of individuals, private foundations, and state programs, the fort began restoring the gardens, a process that would take nine years. Crumbling brick eroded by harsh northern winters was painstakingly repaired. Pathways were cleared of years of weeds and brushy overgrowth. Original garden ornaments, corroded by exposure to the harsh elements, were refurbished. 'Frau Karl Druschki', a white hybrid

perpetual rose from Coffin's original design, was found barely alive among the weeds and now thrives as it did in the 1920s. A Victorian-style Lord and Burnham greenhouse adjacent to the walled garden once housed thousands of annual seedlings each spring; the antique structure is now being restored.

Coffin's original vision was recreated as accurately as possible, down to the exact location, species, and flower color, based on information from historic photos, personal letters, and magazine articles. Long-lost heirloom varieties were rediscovered in Cornell University's collection of 1920s seed catalogs. The height or flower color of some varieties had changed over the years, so ones that more closely resemble the original plants were substituted. The garden was re-opened to the public in the summer of 2001.

Modifications to the original plan were inevitable. Coffin's design was typical of the Gilded Age, when the wealthy planted whatever they wanted and employed a bevy of full-time gardeners. Today, the garden is tended by one full-time landscape curator and relies heavily on seasonal help and volunteers. The present design incorporates reliable perennials and modern hybrids for less labor-intensive maintenance. The King's Garden is now returned to its former glory, a sparkling crown jewel in a majestic setting. ❧

*S*ome of the most innovative gardens in the world are created by artists. French Impressionist Claude Monet was known as much for his gardens as he was for his paintings. Many plots in the Adirondacks are cultivated by local artists, relying on their natural talent to paint, weave, or sculpt a horticultural masterpiece. Many see the garden as an empty canvas, the focus not on individual cultivars but on form, colors, and texture. Some don't even know the botanical or common names, instead planting with a painter's eye and creative instinct. The result is breathtaking beauty interjected with personal touches, endearing quirks, and an element of surprise.

Artists and Their Gardens

A Weaver's Garden

For Wilmington artist Annoel Krider, weaving is the perfect training ground for creating tapestries of a horticultural sort. Krider has designed and tended gardens at Whiteface Golf Course, where her husband is a golf pro, as well as various private gardens in the area. Her mountainside cabin rises from the steep hillside like a chalet in the Swiss Alps. The window of her ground-floor studio perfectly frames a cottage-style garden and dramatic mountain backdrop.

Winding paths more suited to nimble mountain goats are carved into the precipitous slope below the house. Puffy clouds of plume poppies (*Macleaya cordata*) glow in the backlight of the waning summer sun. Spikes of blue delphinium and stately hollyhocks contrast with the huge, rounded leaves of butterbur (*Petasites japonicus*) and mounds of ground-hugging pinks (*Dianthus*).

For her garden, Krider transfers her weaving sensibilities to creating free-form trellises crafted from intertwining twigs. These garden structures were a natural progression from her weaving, where she often incorporates painted twigs into her pictorial and Southwestern-style tapestries. The trellises and

Pathways wind throughout Annoel Krider's garden.

arbors, which support plants such as sweetly scented trumpet honeysuckle *(Lonicera sempervirens)*, signify transitions into different parts of the garden or are simply ornamental.

Krider gardens organically, using no chemicals, and amends the soil with compost from the Lake Placid horse show grounds. The hillside garden is home to a diverse collection of cottage-style flowering plants: iris, mallow, peonies, speedwell, black-eyed Susan, yarrow, daisies, Maltese cross, and lavender. Krider experiments with many roses and has had success with several English varieties, including 'Iceberg' and the climber 'Blaze'. Magenta blooms of rose campion *(Lychnis coronaria)* are welcome self-sown volunteers up and down the slope. Purple coneflowers are magnets for nectar-seeking butterflies and hummingbirds.

In the woods along the driveway, a shade garden framed by a rustic stone wall is home to ligularia, ferns, hostas, coral bells, butterbur, and daylilies. A recently added wildflower garden below the driveway is reminiscent of an alpine meadow and offers dramatic views of nearby Bassett and Wainwright Mountains in the distance.

Above: Weaver Annoel Krider's cabin overlooks her garden.

Below: Drifts of flowers frame the view from the cabin.

Hollyhocks (above) and trumpet honeysuckle (right) in the Krider garden

Of Sculpture and Whimsy

Just off the sleepy main street of Bloomingdale is a horticultural gem created by Ralph and Bernadette Prata. Ralph is a well-known local artist, selling his concrete sculptures in shows around the country. Several cats adopted from the local shelter are an integral part of the garden, leading visitors on their own personal tours. Bernadette began the gardens by hauling in yards of manure and other organic matter to amend the soil. In place of a lawn, the front yard is a lush tapestry of prolifically blooming daylilies, bee balm, campanulas, mullein, hydrangeas, ferns, and Oriental and Asiatic lilies. The porch is home to potted cactus and other tender houseplants that spend the winter indoors.

A rustic twig fence and arbor frame the central garden in back of the house. Tibetan prayer flags, which are thought to bring happiness, long life, and pros-

Ralph Prata created the cement sculptures throughout the garden.

Right: On a breezy day, Tibetan prayer flags add lively movement to the Prata garden.

Below: Stately hollyhocks in the main garden are complemented by a rustic twig fence.

perity, are strung between the house and the garage, which serves as Ralph's studio. The garden is exuberant and loosely designed, with stately plantings of hollyhock, black-eyed Susan, Asiatic and Oriental lilies, and annual sunflowers with blooms the size of dinner plates. A flower bed in front of the two-story garage is home to a climbing trumpet honeysuckle *(Lonicera sempervirens)*, globe thistle, ferns, and tiger lilies.

The garden is filled with examples of artistic whimsy. Ralph's cement sculptures lend themselves as outdoor garden art, harmonizing with the surrounding plants. Antique tools and watering cans, twig wall hangings, brightly painted birdhouses, and various pieces of metalwork adorn the studio, house, and gardens. A nylon clothesline playfully strung between two posts resembles old power lines. Wind chimes and snowshoes adorn a lean-to garden shed.

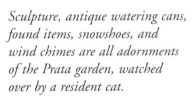

*Sculpture, antique watering cans,
found items, snowshoes, and
wind chimes are all adornments
of the Prata garden, watched
over by a resident cat.*

An Artists' Oasis

One of the finest gardens in the Adirondacks lies near the town of Malone. Artists Charlie Atwood-King and Karen Lamitie-King created a series of garden rooms in each diverse aspect of the property: open clearing, deeply shaded woods, and babbling brook. Karen, who taught art to elementary school students in the Malone school district for thirty years, is retired and creates paintings and multimedia images while tending the vast gardens. Charlie, a counselor

at a local corrections facility, finds personal balance by creating art in a remarkable array of mediums.

Even though Malone is north of the frigid High Peaks region, the climate is somewhat warmer because of the lower elevation. Karen and Charlie purchased the ten-acre property primarily for the deep, rushing brook in back of the house. They wanted a home with a timeless feel and settled on building an 1800s saltbox-style house. There are distinctly Adirondack features as well, including twig railings, rough log

supports, and screened porches made for summer sitting and sleeping. Across from the house is a large barn, which serves as an artist's studio.

The buildings' dark green siding with deep red trim is a perfect backdrop for the exuberant perennial borders and kitchen garden along the front of the house. The borders, planned for peak bloom in July, spill forth with sky blue towers of delphinium, graceful stands of hollyhock, perennial sunflowers, bee balm, black-eyed Susans, and daisies. Karen starts all of the perennials from seed. In July, she direct-sows new varieties in nursery beds and lets them overwinter for two years before transplanting them into their final places.

Charlie's finely honed artistic expertise includes painting, weaving, and furniture making. His Impressionist Adirondack landscapes draw rave reviews in regional gallery shows and are in many private collections. The house is amply furnished with his museum-quality Mission-style and Adirondack twig pieces. Charlie's woodworking skills extend into the

Facing page: Weathered clapboards are a perfect backdrop for a bright mix of old-fashioned hollyhocks.

Above: A Mission-style bench lends a romantic feel to the King garden.

Below: Perennial borders extend from the house to the studio.

garden, which is filled with rustic trellises, fences, gates, arbors, and benches. At the garden entrance, a purple clematis clambers up one side of the rustic gate. A large double arbor leads visitors to an expansive veranda. Along the front of the house, a split post fence with twig detailing lends a backdrop to the free-flowing perennial borders.

Roses have to be tough to survive here; favorites include Canadian Explorers 'John Cabot', 'Champlain', and 'William Baffin'. The latter is exceptionally hardy and is trained as a climber on a rustic trellis along the porch. Others include rugosas and wild cottage roses dug up from roadsides.

In summer, the brook is a favorite gathering spot, with seating areas placed along the banks. A rustic gazebo lined with thick cushions is a favorite place to have early-morning coffee. Between the house and brook is a moon garden with all-white flowers, seating, and ornaments. At night, light reflects off the ivory-colored surfaces, casting a soft glow.

Behind the house, an herb garden is flanked by a rustic arbor seat and a greenhouse made from salvaged materials, including old windows and a door. In early spring, the glasshouse bulges with trays of

Top: 'William Baffin' is one of several hardy roses in the King garden.

Center: The rustic gazebo is the perfect setting for an afternoon nap.

Bottom: The garden beckons visitors to make a leisurely stroll to the 1800s-style saltbox house.

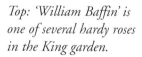

tender annual and perennial seedlings. In summer, once the seedlings have been planted out, it becomes an outdoor living room, complete with plush chairs and couch, carpeting, coffee table, artwork, and a grand chandelier. On sunny winter days, the closed greenhouse is warm enough to sit in.

Each summer, friends of kindred creative spirit are invited to an "Artists in the Garden" event. Each guest paints, draws, sculpts, or photographs a work inspired by the garden, and the resulting creations are displayed at the Visitor Interpretive Center in Paul Smiths the following fall.

Top left: Local painter Tim Fortune paints at the annual Artists in the Garden event.

Above and left: In summer, the greenhouse is transformed into an outdoor living room.

The studio's spare, clean lines complement the garden's rich color and detail.

Rustic arbors, trellises and fences built by Charlie Atwood-King are found throughout the garden.

Kenjockety

Westport, a small town known for its historic waterfront and grand Victorian homes, is nestled on the southwestern shore of Lake Champlain. Not far from town along a quiet lakeshore drive is the estate of Kenjockety. The twenty-acre property is the summer home and studio of two New York City artists who find creative inspiration and spiritual renewal in this pastoral setting. The gardens, which emphasize form, structure, and texture, reflect their artistry.

The Prairie-style house, unusual architecture for this area, is clearly out of its element. The house was built in 1910 by a homesick Midwesterner from Wisconsin who married a local woman. Outbuildings include a large barn, which now serves as an artist's studio, and a boathouse, which doubles as a waterfront studio. The current owners bought the property in 1985 and have made extensive renovations to the house and grounds.

Much of the hardscape and structure of the garden,

Above: Asiatic lilies at Kenjockety

Below: A garden room is surrounded with lush plantings of perennials.

Left: A blue lattice fence echoes the color of the sky.

Below: A dense cedar grove is underplanted with hosta, ginger, and woodland ferns.

including the arbors, terraces, and major plantings, were designed by the late Dan Kiley, a renowned landscape architect based in Charlotte, Vermont. His best-known projects include the Gateway Arch in St. Louis, the John F. Kennedy Library in Boston, and the East Wing of the National Gallery in Washington, D.C.

The gardens surrounding the house are understated, reflecting Kiley's minimalist style, with a distinctly Asian influence. The emphasis is not on flowers but on individual elements—a simple sculpture, a stone urn, a flagstone patio, or a lone bench—that lead the eye to the surrounding scenery of lake and forest.

A path leads from the house through a small, dense grove of cedars, the thick canopy beautifully underplanted with drifts of hosta, wild ginger *(Asarum europaeum)*, and native ferns. The path continues past the studio along a wooded trail and through a grove of sumacs before arriving at the principal gardens.

The flat terrain is broken into several garden rooms, which allow the visitor to stop and reflect on each area. The vistas here are grand, and the gardens are innovatively brought into the scale of the landscape. At the entrance to the garden, a thirty-foot-long arbor with thick stone columns is covered with long flower clusters of Japanese wisteria *(Wisteria floribunda)* in June. The braided four-inch trunks twine up each pillar, the thick vines nearly smothering the lattice roof. Wisteria are marginal this far north; this planting, which took twelve years to flower, is arguably the most spectacular in the Adirondacks. Although the foliage is lush, the bloom varies widely from year to year—sometimes sparse and other times profuse.

The arbor forms one side of a formal garden room enclosed with a cedar hedge. A wide expanse of lawn is flanked with English-style perennial borders planted with tall stands of bugbane *(Actaea simplex* 'Brunette'), meadow rue *(Thalictrum)*, asters, Asiatic lilies, astilbe, coral bells, alliums, lady's mantle *(Alchemilla mollis)*, gayfeather, phlox, and hills-of-snow hydrangea *(Hydrangea arborescens* 'Grandiflora'). Low, simple stone benches at either end of the garden room offer a place to sit. A stone seat in the center has a shallow bowl that catches rainwater and reflects the sky.

An adjacent garden room has an open border, loosely defined by a blue lattice fence. A screen of weeping willows *(Salix babylonica)* breaks the view between the garden and a large expanse of fields. In spring, a long row of peonies at one side bursts into early-season color. Directly across from the peonies, a

Native ferns soften the foundation of the Prairie-style home at Kenjockety (right), where gardens blend seamlessly with the surrounding woods (above).

long hedge of peegee hydrangeas lends late-season color with creamy white blossoms that fade to pink. The mixed borders are planted with Asiatic lilies, purple-leaved ninebark *(Physocarpus opulifolius* 'Diabolo'), ligularia, white coneflower *(Echinacea purpurea* 'White Swan'), campanula, phlox, and sturdy roses. 'Champlain' and 'William Baffin', two Canadian Explorer roses, are exceptionally hardy; the latter can be trained as a climber. 'Nearly Wild', with single pink blooms all season long, is one of the few floribunda roses that performs well in cold climates. The thick, architectural leaves of colewort *(Crambe cordifolia)* support clouds of white blossoms reminiscent of baby's breath. Although listed as hardy only to USDA Zone

6, it thrives in this protected spot. Several varieties of clematis, including creamy white 'Henryi' and carmine red 'Ville de Lyon', meander along the lattice fence.

Adjacent to the two main garden rooms, several rows of grapes are flanked by 'Statuesque' daylilies, an unusually tall variety with bright yellow flowers that reaches five feet. Beyond the formally planted gardens is an expansive space defined by the contrasting forms of rounded, arching weeping willow and a long row of stately poplars. The field is filled with wildflowers, including milkweed, which attracts a large population of monarch butterflies in late summer and early fall.

The gardens are designed to have foliage or flower interest from spring to fall. In May, more than 8,000 bulbs complement the perennial plantings of peonies and wisteria. Late-season bloomers include aster and bugbane. The large grove of sumac provides a spectacular backdrop of crimson red foliage in fall. ❦

Left: An ornate iron bench at Kenjockety rests on pavers softened by tufts of lawn.

Above: The perennial border of one garden room blooms with subtle colors of cream, gold, and burgundy.

ike the early settlers before them, Adirondack gardeners today struggle to produce a bountiful harvest. The short growing season and fluctuating temperatures place undue stress on tender vegetable plants, weakening their ability to produce normal yields. Many warm-weather plants such as tomatoes, bell peppers, corn, and eggplant don't have enough warm days to grow fruit that is fully ripe or large enough. Thin, rocky, or sandy soils must be richly amended to support crops. Despite the challenges, Adirondack gardeners do bring in crops of delectable vegetables, greens, and fruits by choosing carefully from traditional cold-tolerant varieties and hardy new hybrids and by strategic placement of their garden beds.

The Edible Garden

Back to Basics

Thomas Akstens of Bakers Mills has been growing vegetables in the Adirondacks for twenty years. When he first moved here from the southern Hudson Valley, he happily planted his favorite varieties and was jolted with the reality of green tomatoes, stunted corn, and finger-size bell peppers. Since then, he has experimented with a wide range of edibles, honing his selections to what performs best. By accepting the limitations of the short season, he has dramatically increased his yields.

Once part of a dairy farm, Aksten's property lies at the base of a mountain, so cold air settles in pockets.

At 1,500 feet in elevation, this USDA Zone 3 garden has only a ninety-day growing season. After years of experimentation with every season-extending gimmick imaginable, Akstens has returned to basics. He starts with good soil and adds lots of compost, leaf mulch, or manure along with a dose of lime.

Warm-weather crops, including tomatoes and eggplant, are started in trays on a wide, south-facing garage windowsill in early March. Cool-weather vegetables, including carrots, cabbage, lettuce, and other leaf crops, are sown in April. By Memorial Day, the seedlings are large enough to be acclimated to the outdoors. Asktens simply carries the trays in and out

Leaf lettuces perform better than head-forming types in short-season climates.

Right: One of several vegetable plots on the Akstens property

Below: Purple and green cabbages planted in neat, artful rows

of the garage, leaving them outside for increasingly longer periods to avoid shock. He plants the seedlings in the ground as early as possible under row covers, which offer several degrees of frost protection as well as defense from most insects. He leaves the covers on all season for leaf crops such as collards and kale.

Because they are easily started from seed and grow quickly, greens are an ideal crop for North Country gardens. Akstens grows a mix of standard leaf lettuces for salads along with heirloom varieties such as the mild-tasting 'Deer Tongue' and the frilly crimson-leaved 'Red Sails'. More exotic Asian greens such as mizuna are tossed with arugula, collards, or chard for a quick and tasty stir-fry. An array of herbs including parsley, dill, thyme, and sage are used to season homemade vegetable dishes. Onions, chives, leeks, shallots, and garlic provide additional flavor.

Akstens provides plenty of supplemental water when the rains won't cooperate, and he fertilizes with water-soluble fish emulsion. He also uses chicken manure, aged so it doesn't burn young seedlings. He's not shy about trying warm-weather crops such as melon, eggplant, and tomatoes. 'Juliet', a small paste tomato, produced ten to fifteen pounds of fruit on a single bush-type plant.

Akstens recently began experimenting with growing vegetables in containers. Dark-colored pots are filled with a mix of sphagnum moss, topsoil, and compost amended with sand, wood ashes, and Plantone. Tomato, eggplant, zucchini, and pepper seedlings, which are started in flats, are transplanted into the containers in May and placed on the south side of the garage. The pots absorb and retain heat from the sun; the building offers extra warmth and protection from the wind. When temperatures dip below 40 degrees

English-style wattle fence in the garden of Pam Doré

Fahrenheit at night, the containers are covered with tarps or moved into the garage with a hand truck. The potted plants grow faster and fruit several weeks earlier than seedlings placed directly in the ground. They also produce over a longer period of time, resulting in larger yields.

Akstens keeps a diary of planting times and weather conditions. He notes the performance of each variety and what can be improved upon the next year. These detailed records are a crucial tool for maximizing success and increasing yields.

A Bountiful Harvest

Adirondack gardeners are constantly looking for ways to extend the growing season. In North Jay, garden designer Pam Doré built a large greenhouse from recycled windows to protect the tender annual flowers she raises for her clients each spring. In late May, the plants are delivered to clients, and the beds inside the greenhouse are planted with warm-season tomatoes and melons. The plants are trained up string trellises to make efficient use of the vertical space. The glass magnifies the heat and accelerates growth, producing

Pam Doré's large vegetable garden is framed by bucolic mountain views.

A large greenhouse made from recycled materials houses tender annuals Doré raises for commercial clients. A café table and two chairs in one corner of the greenhouse offer a place to enjoy a cup of tea.

an earlier, more robust crop. The greenhouse is equipped with a small woodstove to make working conditions more comfortable on cold early-spring days. A café table and two chairs in one corner offer a place to relax and enjoy a cup of tea.

A large vegetable garden between the greenhouse and barn produces ample food for a family of two; surplus is shared with neighbors and friends. The long rows and pathways are kept in the same configuration each year to keep the beds from being compacted by foot traffic. Composted chicken and horse manure are worked into the soil each year along with an application of Perk, which adds essential trace minerals. Seedlings are grown in the greenhouse in early spring and placed outside when the danger of frost is past.

Warm-weather crops of eggplant, beans, squash, peppers, and basil are placed toward the front of the garden, where they receive the most warmth. A diverse selection of onions, cabbage, kale, lettuce, and cauliflower ensures a bountiful harvest even in cool, wet seasons. At the rear of the garden, a wattle fence, an ancient style made popular in England, supports vining squash and tomatoes. The trellises keep fruit from lying on the ground and make it easier to harvest. Slow-drip soaker hoses reduce the amount of evaporation when watering.

Doré intersperses tried-and-true vegetables with unusual varieties, including French green beans; Armenian, English, and lemon cucumbers; and 'Climbing Trombocino', a trumpet-shaped Italian summer squash with an artichoke-like flavor.

Tried and True

Lake Clear, located northwest of Saranac Lake, is in one of the coldest areas of the Adirondacks, with –30 degree Fahrenheit winter temperatures not uncommon. Raising food crops is especially tough in this USDA Zone 3 region. Frosts can occur in any month of the year, and the growing season is just ninety days. Dana Fast has practiced the art of raising vegetables here for thirty years, growing most of the produce she eats year-round. She freezes much of her crop and grows varieties of winter squash, potatoes, and other root vegetables that store well for long periods. Her asparagus patch has produced a bumper crop for twenty-eight years.

Like many Adirondack gardeners, Fast uses only organic methods, shunning toxic pesticides or chemical fertilizers. Through methodical trial and error, she has increased her yields by learning which varieties perform best. She's attuned to the fine nuances of coaxing the best out of each cultivar, responding to the ever-changing needs of the plants by instinct. In order to broaden her choices, Fast prefers growing plants from seed rather than buying starts. Most of her seed comes from Johnny's Selected Seeds, Stokes, and Burpee, all of which offer varieties for cold climates.

Though she enjoys trying new cultivars, she mostly sticks with tried-and-true varieties.

In the last week of February, Fast sets up grow-lights in her basement and sows seed for the plants that take longest to grow: leeks, celery root, and bell peppers (including 'Ace', red 'Jingle Bells', and 'Gypsy'). Her rudimentary but functional setup involves eight shop-light fixtures fitted with a combination of cool- and warm-spectrum fluorescent tubes, which she finds work better than specially made (and more expensive) grow-lights. The lights are positioned four to six inches above seed trays set on shelves; the correct distance prevents plants from becoming leggy.

Early March is when Fast starts petunias, snapdragons, and alpine strawberries from seed. She sows the majority of vegetables during the third week in March along with some flowers. Tomato, cabbage, self-blanching cauliflower, and Brussels sprouts seedlings grow alongside ornamentals such as flowering tobacco (*Nicotiana*) and zinnias.

The soil in Fast's garden is sandy, rocky, and acid. She adds loads of horse manure from a local farm to the vegetable beds each year, and works wood ashes into the soil if the pH drops below 6.5. A cover crop of crimson clover provides an extra boost of nitrogen.

Dana Fast's asparagus patch (left side of photo) has produced bumper crops for twenty-eight years.

Left: Despite the exceptionally short growing season of Lake Clear, Dana Fast usually manages to raise productive tomato plants (at right in photo).

Below: Green beans from the Fast garden

Two cold frames allow her to direct-sow early crops of lettuce and radishes in late April. (At the other end of the growing season, the frames shelter thicker-leaved varieties of lettuce such as romaine and cold-weather types of spinach. In most years, these can be started as late as September for a November harvest.)

In mid-May, the real work begins. Fast direct-seeds carrots, beets, parsnips, turnips, snap peas, and snow peas into the 1,800-square-foot garden. Direct-seeded broccoli supplements the plants already started indoors. She covers the crops with floating row covers to warm the soil and protect tender seedlings from root maggots and other pests.

Successive plantings of direct-seeded leaf crops from

May until September ensure a continuous harvest. Fast grows a wide range of leafy vegetables, including bok choy and other Asian greens, spinach, kale (including curly Siberian), and colorful 'Brite Lites' Swiss chard. Leaf lettuces perform better than head-forming types in this climate.

The ultimate challenge is to produce a plump, juicy red tomato before the first frost. Fast's favorite for salads is Burpee's 'Early Pick', which ripens in sixty-two days and has good flavor, solid flesh, and resistance to wilt. 'New Yorker', a bush type that ripens in sixty-five days, is a vigorous grower with heavy yields. Named for its yellow color, 'Taxi' produces fruit with a meaty texture and sweet flavor in sixty-four days. A favorite variety that is new for her is 'Juliet', ripening in just sixty days, with small, elongated fruits and a sweet taste. The vines keep producing until frost.

At planting time, Fast lays the bottom six to eight inches of each tomato plant in a shallow trench and covers it with soil. Roots sprout along the length of the buried stem, resulting in a more vigorous root system. The top six inches of soil warm quickly, so young seedlings get an extra boost from being planted close to the surface. Black plastic spread around tomatoes and peppers absorbs additional heat from the sun. Floating row covers protect warm-weather crops until mid-June and intermittently throughout the growing season on exceptionally cool nights or at the first sign of frost.

Farmers' Markets: Growing Local

These days, the average person in the United States can buy nearly any kind of vegetable or fruit year-round in the local grocery store. Yet concerns over freshness combined with less regulation of pesticides and chemicals in other countries have more Americans returning to local farmers for their food.

Farmers' markets are a way for consumers and growers to come together without the middleman of the grocery store. This personal contact facilitates community and personal relationships, and consumers feel more connected to where their food comes from. Local farmers can reap higher profits (and therefore stand a better chance of surviving in the age of megafarms). In turn, consumers are assured of fresh, high-quality produce.

There are many farmers' markets in the Adirondacks, including those in Elizabethtown, Keene, Westport, Saranac Lake, and Malone. Many of the markets also include special events such as crafts fairs and harvest festivals. See page 176 in Resources for additional information. ✣

Valley View Farm in Saranac sells homemade jams, honey, soap, and candles as well as cut flowers.

*Maple products, fresh
corn, beets, 'Brite Lites'
Swiss chard, and carrots
from Rivermede Farm
in Keene Valley*

Gardens of the Southern Adirondacks

Restoring a Terraced Garden

The Caroga region is located in the sparsely populated southernmost fringe of the Adirondack Park. When Barbara McMartin and her husband bought their home on Canada Lake in 1994, the picturesque lakeside location wasn't the only enticement. McMartin, a well-known regional writer, was just as intrigued with an old terraced garden hidden by years of overgrowth on the steep slope across the road. That garden was created in the 1920s by the Tyoe family, who once operated the 1890s camp as an inn.

After transforming the rustic cottage into a comfortable year-round home, McMartin turned her attention to the neglected slope. She pulled out and pruned a tangle of vines, weeds, and trees to reveal a semicircular amphitheater of terraced pathways and stone staircases. The south-facing hillside, sheltered

Top: Rich bronze colors light up the Millman-Taft garden in fall.

Right: Barbara McMartin artfully juxtaposes contrasting foliage, shapes, and textures.

Barbara McMartin's slope garden looks out onto Canada Lake.

from harsh winter winds, is bathed with filtered light. The stone walls and pathways absorb the sun's rays, heating the soil. In winter, when the plants die back, the stones poking through the snow cover provide architectural interest.

The terraces were cleaned up and railings were added to assist visitors up and down the narrow stone pathways. Traversing the precarious pathways is reminiscent of a vigorous mountain hike on a High Peaks trail. A fence around the entire perimeter ensures that prized plants won't be eaten by deer. Unfortunately, the fence is no deterrent to chipmunks, which are worse in some years than others. They dig

holes, yanking plants from their anchored spots and destroying the roots.

The garden, a work in progress, showcases the unusual perennials that McMartin avidly collects from around the country. She tucks treasured specimens into cracks and crevices; each succeeding terrace reveals a new surprise. Years of decomposed leaf mulch from the surrounding woods make the soil naturally rich. Native woodland plants collected from a privately owned property include trillium, Solomon's seal, anemone, and ferns. In late spring, the hillside is covered with regal stands of self-sowing foxglove (white, purple, and pink shades of *Digitalis purpurea).*

McMartin favors plants with foliage interest, including coral bells, bishop's hat *(Epimedium),* hosta, lungwort, lady's mantle *(Alchemilla mollis),* and Japanese painted fern *(Athyrium nipponicum* 'Pictum'), with its burgundy red stems and frosted leaves. Astilbe, several hues of bleeding heart, spiderwort, columbine, and campanula offer a rich carpet of long-blooming flowers. A large semicircular garden at the bottom of the slope is open and gets more light, so sun-loving

Coral bells (Heuchera), *hostas, and lungwort* (Pulmonaria) *show off a variety of striped, speckled, and deeply veined leaves.*

daylilies, lupine, peonies, iris, black-eyed Susan, and phlox thrive here. A favorite plant is the exceptionally hardy queen-of-the-prairie *(Filipendula rubra)*, with feathery pink blooms and deeply serrated leaves.

In spring, hundreds of yellow and white daffodils bloom up and down the terraced slope. Lenten rose *(Helleborus orientalis)* begins flowering almost as soon as the snow melts and continues until early summer. Purple, pink, and blue asters complemented by tall stands of Joe Pye weed and Japanese anemone offer late-season color.

A Colonial Hamlet in the Adirondacks

In the village of Corinth, retired schoolteachers Phil and Mary Baugh re-created a New England village inspired by trips to Sturbridge Village in Massachusetts, the Shelburne Museum in Vermont, and Colonial Williamsburg in Virginia. Their three-acre homestead includes a one-room schoolhouse, general store, tavern, blacksmith shop, Colonial kitchen, and smokehouse, all furnished with antiques collected over the past thirty years. The design of an unusual octagonal potting shed dates to 1740, and a New Hampshire–style gazebo is similar to those built in 1850.

Perennial gardens already flanked the house when the Baughs bought the Colonial-style home in 1970.

When they retired in the mid-1990s, they began adding more flower beds and built several large ponds rimmed with local stone. Between the house and the 1880 saltbox carriage barn are exuberant mixed borders. Antique farm tools are decoratively displayed on the front of the barn. A white picket fence provides an attractive backdrop to the cottage-style borders. Four ponds and waterfalls are home to koi and other fish. Native birds and wildlife are frequent visitors; Phil has spotted more than forty-five species of birds.

The gardens are designed to bloom over three sea-

Above: The Baughs' Colonial-style buildings are furnished with period antiques.

Left: A carriage barn is the backdrop for the expansive perennial borders in the Baugh garden.

sons. In spring, daffodils, primroses, and iris bring the garden to life. Cottage-style summer perennials include phlox, purple coneflower, yarrow, gayfeather, bee balm, and perennial sunflower. By fall, ornamental grasses, Russian sage, asters, and peegee hydrangea offer late-season color. Golden clematis *(Clematis tangutica)*, rarely seen in Adirondack gardens, has an unusual yellow bloom and is normally hardy only to USDA Zone 6. A large weeping pine *(Pinus strobus* 'Pendula') near the main pond offers a striking architectural focal point and year-round color. Another treasured specimen is a pitcher plant *(Sarracenia purpurea)* that was rescued from a roadside construction site. One of just two carnivorous Adirondack plants, *Sarracenia* is extremely hardy, to USDA Zone 2. The flowers are variable, ranging from purple to green.

The Baughs decided to share their passions for history and gardening and in 2002 opened their property to the public. For a nominal fee, visitors can enjoy a guided tour and a glimpse of what life was like more than 200 years ago. The property will be left to the town of Corinth, with the hope that it will be turned into a museum.

Below: In the Baughs' water garden, four ponds and waterfalls are home to koi and other fish.

Above: A magnificent clump of fall-blooming Joe Pye weed stands ten feet tall.

Victorian Grandeur at Saratoga Rose

The Saratoga Rose Inn & Restaurant is a well-known landmark in the town of Hadley. The 1885 Victorian house, a soft beige color with pink trim, is an imposing sight to visitors coming up the long gravel driveway. Anthony and Nancy Merlino purchased the house in 1988 and immediately began renovating the building and grounds. The inn has six guest rooms and a full-service restaurant that serves dinner to guests and the general public.

The stately building is surrounded with large old shade trees, imparting a sense of timelessness. The garden beds along the front veranda are thickly planted with hostas, native ferns, and other shade-loving plants. Oversize classic urns lining the staircase are planted with spiky dracaenas surrounded by annual impatiens.

The most spectacular features of the garden are the huge specimens of peegee hydrangeas along the front of the house. In late summer, the elegant vase-shaped shrubs are covered with enormous creamy white flowers that fade to pink. Photos of the house dating to

Above and right: The gardens at Saratoga Rose Inn. The peegee hydrangeas flanking the formal stairs date to the 1930s.

The inn's backyard is often the setting for small, intimate weddings.

the 1930s show the newly planted hydrangea bushes when they were chest high.

During fair weather, guests can dine on the front veranda overlooking the front gardens and a classic two-tiered fountain. The formal beds are an old-fashioned mix of peonies, daylilies, gayfeather, phlox, gooseneck loosestrife, and spirea.

In 1996, the Merlinos added gardens in back of the house, complete with a gazebo, pond, and seating areas. The setting is often used for small, intimate wedding ceremonies. The elevated lawn area between the house and gardens was the site of a large glass greenhouse, which was torn down. It's thought that dances were held inside the glasshouse.

A formal brick pathway leads from the house to the rear gardens. The two-level pond and connecting waterfall are built with native stones that are softened with native ferns, impatiens, and Hakone grass (*Hakonechloa macra* 'Aureola'). The mixed border contains easy-care perennials, conifers, shrubs, and annual nasturtiums. The adjacent lawn is adorned with island plantings of hosta and stands of white birch, as well as boulders, small benches, and Adirondack chairs.

In 2004, the Saratoga Rose Inn & Restaurant was sold to Richard Ferrugio and Claude Belanger. They plan on observing the gardens for a full growing season before making any major changes, although they will add hundreds of spring-blooming bulbs to the front and rear gardens.

A Shared Devotion to Gardening

Daylilies are a mainstay of North Country gardens, and Sally Millman-Taft and her husband, Dr. Russell Taft, devoted their gardening lives to growing them. Their property on Route 149 in Queensbury was filled with beds dedicated to cataloguing and hybridizing every type, from doubles to spiders. In the late 1980s, the beds were expanded to include other plants and were gradually developed into more organized and designed gardens.

Dr. Taft spent his last days at the Fort Hudson Nursing Home in Fort Edward, and Millman-Taft was instrumental in developing gardens at the facility. She also continued to expand her own gardens, holding open houses several times a year. The open garden weekends were a cause for celebration, with cool refreshments, classical music, and lots of plant talk. The evening before each tour, friends came to cut back spent blooms; these "deadheading parties" often turned festive. Millman-Taft took great pleasure in inspiring others to realize what they could accomplish in USDA Zone 4 gardens.

Most of the gardens were designed by Millman-Taft (a retired sixth-grade teacher at Kensington Road School in Glens Falls), and she devised a twenty-year

plan for the property. She enlisted the help of Glens Falls garden designer Greg Greene and ecologist Drew Monthie, who assisted in restoring a twenty-acre meadow and wetlands adjacent to the main property.

The sandy loam was amended with peat moss, bonemeal, blood meal, and granular Plantone, an organic fertilizer. A mulch of fine bark helped control weeds and retain moisture. Extensive hardscaping of

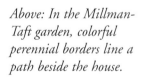

Above: In the Millman-Taft garden, colorful perennial borders line a path beside the house.

Right: Black-eyed Susan, sedums, tickseed (Coreopsis), and purple coneflower are planted among mainstay daylilies.

rock walls, pathways, arbors, and terraces was added to enhance the existing structure of the original trees and shrubs.

The garden along the side of the house is the most colorful, with drifts of daylilies in every shade imaginable interspersed with gayfeather, white and purple coneflower *(Echinacea purpurea)*, black-eyed Susan, tickseed, and self-sowing *Verbena bonariensis*. A cement birdbath and twig trellises add focal points.

The front of the house has sweeping vistas of meadows and the Green Mountains of Vermont. Ornamental grasses, which are underutilized in Adirondack gardens, are used here to great effect. The island beds in the main lawn were planted with towering perennials such as Joe Pye weed, eulalia grass *(Miscanthus sinensis* 'Gracillimus'), and purple moor grass (Molinia caerulea 'Skyracer'). Several varieties of Japanese maple *(Acer palmatum)* thrive here, providing a backdrop of spectacular crimson color.

A patio inlaid with small brick pavers provides a comfortable seating area next to a crescent-shaped pond. The waters are lush with arrowhead *(Sagittaria)*, water lilies, rushes, and yellow flag *(Iris pseudacorus)*. Millman-Taft loved to collect garden art of all kinds; Oriental statues, bronze turtles, and abstract sculptures are found throughout the gardens.

Unfortunately, Millman-Taft would not see her twenty-year plan to fruition. She passed away in September 2001 after a short illness. The gardens are being tended by her niece, preserving the legacy left by a devoted couple who clearly loved their little piece of heaven in the Adirondacks.

Sculptures enhace the extraordinary gardens Sally Millman-Taft enjoyed sharing with others.

Warrensburg in Bloom

In Warrensburg, six miles northwest of Lake George village, vintage storefronts and elegant Victorian homes line the main street. The town is known for its antiques shops and the self-proclaimed World's Largest Garage Sale in October, which draws thousands of people each year. The town beautification committee, founded in 1984, maintains the colorful public plantings at the Chamber of Commerce, town hall, bandstand, and several local parks. The non-profit organization works with volunteers and youth groups to design and maintain the seasonal displays: early spring bulbs, summer annuals, fall decorations, and holiday lights. Local business owners get into the act, too. Dentist Raluca Sandler plants flowers in front of her office building and maintains a large garden adjacent to the back parking lot. Just up the street, the Cornerstone Victorian B&B incorporated established plantings with a new garden created by local designer Kerry Mendez.

Right: Mixed borders of iris, daylilies, sedums, artemisia, perennial sunflower, yarrow, and bee balm along the pathway to the Whalen house

Below: The Japanese-style teahouse

A Japanese Garden, Adirondack Style

Warrensburg Beautification Committee member Teresa Whalen, who is also active in the Adirondack Mountain Garden Club, maintains her garden on a property atop Harrington Hill. The site has commanding views of the town and surrounding mountains. An eclectic mix of Adirondack and Japanese style, the house and gardens were inspired by husband Raymond's time in Japan during the Korean War.

The garden accommodates the natural limitations of rocky outcroppings, steep slopes, and deep woodland shade. Plants are selected for hardiness and sited according to microclimate: open, windy areas; sheltered woods; or a sunny southern exposure. The surroundings of forest, mountains, and native plants are incorporated into the garden's design. Attached to the

home is a Japanese-style teahouse built by Raymond; here the Whalens linger over meals or a cup of coffee on summer days. The sight of the teahouse, perched on a rock ledge with dramatic mountain backdrops, is reminiscent of an ancient Japanese tapestry. Eight stone lanterns placed throughout the property were discovered at auctions and antiques stores.

The Whalens designed the garden to have something blooming from early spring until fall. Many cultivars are Japanese in origin, including Kousa dogwood *(Cornus kousa* 'Milky Way'), Japanese flowering crab apple *(Malus floribunda)*, and Japanese painted

fern *(Athyrium nipponicum* 'Pictum'). Large mixed borders of iris, daylilies, sedums, artemisia, perennial sunflower, yarrow, and bee balm line a curved pathway that leads to the house.

The rocky soil is mainly loam. Manure and compost are dug into the flower beds, and perennials are top-dressed with organic mulch. In fall, plants are left uncut to provide a food source of seeds and berries for wildlife and to offer winter interest.

An Adirondack-style garden shed built by Raymond is painted green and brown to blend with the surroundings and decorated with birch bark flower boxes. At one corner of the shed, two climbing hydrangeas *(Hydrangea petiolaris)* have grown their tendrils to the roof. Near the driveway, a small outbuilding is surrounded with hosta, hydrangea, and native ferns. Local old-timers say the structure was once a radio shack used to communicate with planes dispatched from the air base in Plattsburgh during World War II.

Left: Eight Japanese lanterns in the Whalen garden were discovered at auctions and antiques stores.

Above: Adirondack chairs on a quiet lawn overlook a spectacular mountain vista.

A Passion for Color

For local dentist Raluca Sandler, gardening is a way to relieve stress and renew herself after a long day at work. She decorates the exterior of her office on Warrensburg's Main Street with colorful flower beds and window boxes. At home, her yard is filled with a dazzling display of perennials, annuals, tropicals, and hardy shrubs. Sandler estimates she plants five thousand annuals each year. She keeps them blooming by adding time-release Osmocote fertilizer to the soil at planting time.

The main feature of her home garden is an impressive water garden that houses a number of colorful koi. The pond is terraced with large rocks that are softened by a green backdrop of weeping birch, ferns, and tall, spiky iris. Moisture-loving perennials such as variegated loosestrife *(Lysimachia punctata* 'Alexander'), ligularia, ferns, and cardinal flower *(Lobelia cardinalis)* are planted along the water's edge. The pond contains a rich tapestry of aquatic plants: water hyacinth *(Eichhornia crassipes)*, arrowhead, lotus, and umbrella grass *(Cyperus albostriatus)*. Hardy varieties

of native water lilies and sweet flag stay in the pond year-round.

Exotic-looking plants such as canna lilies, elephant's ear *(Colocasia)*, and *Crocosmia* 'Lucifer' create a tropical look. In fall, Sandler digs up the tropicals and the most tender water plants and overwinters them in the house until the next spring. The fish stay in the pond year-round; a pump and heater keep the water from freezing. The fish hibernate through the winter, so feeding is halted in October and resumed in April.

Right: Black-eyed Susan and gayfeather are a winning combination.

Left: The water feature in Raluca Sandler's garden

Below: The cutting garden includes vibrant zinnias and snapdragons.

The tiny curbside front yard at Kaena Peterson's B&B is a mix of annual, perennial, and tropical plants.

A Taste of Hawaii

The tropical islands of Hawaii are a long way from the tough climate of the Adirondacks, but Kaena Peterson has managed to merge rustic with exotic in her Warrensburg garden. A Hawaiian native who was once a hula dancer at the Tiki Motor Inn in Lake George, Peterson recently opened the Adirondack Victorian B&B. The tiny curbside front yard is a mix of annual, perennial, and tropical plants. The borders along the front of the porch are planted with typical Adirondack staples: orange daylilies, native ferns, and sturdy cinquefoil. Colorful hanging baskets and pots are brimming with petunias, million bells *(Calibrachoa)*, and annual geraniums. Canna lilies, elephant's ear *(Colocasia)*, sweet potato vine *(Ipomoea batatas)*, and coleus, with its brightly colored leaves, lend a tropical feel. The backyard garden is filled with the sound of rushing water from a natural-looking waterfall; perennial borders rim an expanse of lush lawn.

A B&B Country Garden

The Country Road Lodge is located near the base of Hickory Hill Ski Area, several miles outside the town of Warrensburg. In 1967, Steve and Sandi Parisi bought the tiny camp with forty acres on the Hudson River and expanded the house, operating it as a ski lodge and bed-and-breakfast since 1974. After a severe flood eroded the riverbank in 1996, coming within twenty feet of their house, the Parisis moved the building farther from the riverbank, which left the landscape scarred and barren. Steve built an attractive stone wall facing the driveway with river rock, adding loads of organic matter to make fluffy raised beds. They planted the border with hosta, gayfeather, conifers, cinquefoil, black-eyed Susan, daylilies, and other plants rescued from the flooded garden. Over the next three years, they expanded the gardens to include an extensive shade border in back and perennial flower beds around the house.

In 2001, the Parisis built an octagonal gazebo and added a 200-square-foot perennial border, designed by Kerry Mendez. The new beds bloom all summer long with vivid hues of blue delphinium, red and orange Asiatic lilies, spirea, catmint, and old-fashioned daylilies. The screened gazebo offers a place for guests to relax and enjoy the gardens while protected from pesky blackflies and mosquitoes.

The woodland border in back of the house is nestled at the edge of the deciduous forest. The beds are planted with shade-loving native ferns, trillium, columbine, hosta, coral bells, spiderwort, iris, and astilbe. Garden sculptures by Hadley artist Bruno LaVerdiere are at once abstract, timeless, and organic.

The house is adorned with window boxes planted with brightly colored annuals. Nemesia, verbena, zinnias, and marigolds are complemented by foliage plants including sweet potato vine *(Ipomoea batatas)*, licorice plant *(Helichrysum)*, and golden creeping Jenny *(Lysimachia nummularia* 'Aurea'). Million bells *(Calibrachoa)*, a relatively new annual related to petunias, blooms prolifically from early summer until frost and needs no deadheading, as do more traditional varieties of petunias.

A cultivated border along a split-rail fence offers a

The lush perennial borders at the Country Road Lodge

The entry gardens at Country Road Lodge

transition from cultivated gardens to the adjacent wildflower meadows, where guests can wander along meandering trails. Many natives are incorporated into the gardens, supporting and attracting butterflies and other beneficial insects, birds, and other fauna. The property is listed as a designated wildlife habitat by the National Wildlife Federation. ❧

A New Generation of Daylilies

Daylilies are a mainstay of northern gardens. With hundreds of varieties to choose from, the decision of which to plant can be daunting. In recent years, breeders have developed repeat bloomers, including the original variety, 'Stella de Oro', which remains one of the most popular. Other recently introduced repeat bloomers include 'Black Eyed Stella', 'Happy Returns', 'Rosy Returns', 'Romantic Returns', 'Big Time Happy', 'Pardon Me', and 'When My Sweetheart Returns'.

The Central Adirondacks

A Quest for the Unusual

Because of the long, harsh winters, many ornamental woody shrubs struggle to survive in the Adirondacks. The challenge suits Diane Golden just fine. A Connecticut transplant, Diane was accustomed to growing a wide range of woody ornamentals in her former garden and wanted to replicate the effect in her new location. In 1998, Diane and her husband, Tom, bought Hilltop, a house on 250 acres at the edge of Little Pond (formerly Hershey Pond), near the town of Thurman. The Goldens first saw the property in the dead of winter and fell in love with the setting and the solitude. They were assured that despite the remote location, the house had running water and a reliable source of electricity. By spring, it became evident that this was not the case: The shallow well was dry and the house was located off the public power grid. The Goldens shrugged off the inconvenience, dug a deeper well, and installed a system of generators that supply the house with electricity.

The 200-year-old farmhouse is rich in history. It

Above: Japanese iris (Iris ensata) *and wildflowers on the shore of Little Pond*

Below: Variegated dogwood (Cornus alba *'Elegantissima' and 'Gouchaultii'*), *ninebark* (Physocarpus opulifolius *'Diabolo'*), *and Katsura tree* (Cercidiphyllum japonicum *'Heronswood Globe'*)

Mums bring a last burst of color to the Goldens' porch in fall.

Autumn sunlight gilds the many-textured foliage of the Goldens' long perennial bed.

was once run as a resort lodge; most of the food served to guests was grown or caught on the property. Rhubarb plants from the original garden can still be found growing in the woods. The 2,000-foot elevation means winter temperatures can be ten degrees lower than in town. Despite the extreme cold and winter winds, Diane experiments with a wide range of plants. Variegated dogwood *(Cornus alba* 'Elegantissima'), black elder *(Sambucus nigra,* listed as hardy to Zone 6), and ninebark *(Physocarpus opulifolius* 'Diabolo', hardy to USDA Zone 2) are collected from mail-order nurseries such as Gossler Farm, Heronswood, and Forestfarm. Katsura tree *(Cercidiphyllum japonicum* 'Heronswood Globe'), a dwarf form that is hardy to USDA Zone 4, has heart-shaped deep purple leaves in spring and summer, followed by brilliant orange-red foliage in fall.

In just three years, Diane has filled the 125-foot-long perennial border near the house with hundreds of bulbs, perennials, and shrubs. The soil is naturally loamy, providing a rich growing medium. She has planted the banks of the pond and stream across the unpaved road with water lovers such as bigleaf ligularia *(Ligularia dentata* 'Desdemona'), Siberian bugloss *(Brunnera macrophylla),* Japanese iris, and hosta. The soil here is sandy, requiring the addition of compost and manure. A collection of heathers near the road prefers the sharp drainage of the sandy soil.

Though the site is located in a cold USDA Zone 4, Diane tries more tender plants such as sea holly *(Eryngium* 'Sapphire Blue'), spurge *(Euphorbia dulcis* 'Chameleon'), butterfly bush *(Buddleia),* and sourwood *(Oxydendrum arboreum),* all recommended for a minimum of USDA Zone 5. A treasured variety is seven-son flower *(Heptacodium miconioides),* relatively new to American gardens. This deciduous shrub, hardy to USDA Zone 5, has attractive peeling bark and fragrant creamy white flowers in late summer and early fall. The long-lasting flower sepals turn pale red later in the season.

Fall brings subtle color to a Katsura tree

A Roadside Attraction

Sally Joiner's garden on Route 8 is a horticultural showplace for locals and tourists traveling through the hamlet of Brant Lake. Many of the hundreds of plants she collected over the years were swapped with neighbors and fellow members of the Adirondack Mountain Garden Club. The tamarack, birch, and maple trees were transplanted from the nearby woods. Year-end sales at area garden centers are a source for bargains, including fifty lilies that Sally bought for a dollar apiece at Wal-Mart.

The spectacular roadside gardens are a rich tapestry of white birch, small conifers, shrubs, and perennials that change throughout the four seasons. In spring, a snowy canopy of flowering almond, Sargent crab apples, and miniature pears cascades above clusters of tulips in pastel shades of apricot, lavender, and pink. The early blooms give way to the cool hues of spiky iris and towering lupine. In midsummer, the colors shift into high gear, with a sizzling palette of red and yellow Asiatic lilies, majestic stands of scarlet hollyhock, and clumps of orange daylilies. Joiner fills in gaps with quick-growing annual zinnias, pansies, and snapdragons.

A tiered water feature sits in the center of a large island bed. Joiner collected the stones for the water garden and edging of the flower beds from area riverbanks and rockslides. The water feature is softened by moss harvested from the adjacent woods and placed where the flow of water keeps it constantly moist. Sedums cascading over the rocks suggest a botanical waterfall. When the weather warms, Joiner adds water hyacinth *(Eichhornia crassipes)*, native pickerel weed *(Pontederia cordata)*, and water lettuce *(Pistia stratiotes)*.

Vertical stands of white birch and rustic arbors, post fences, and low rock walls form the "bones," or structure, of the garden. Several purple-leaved smoke trees *(Cotinus coggygria)*, marginal in some parts of the Adirondacks, thrive here, growing five to seven feet in a season. Joiner prunes them back hard each year.

Water feature in the Joiner garden

The twenty-year-old cottage-style garden was designed for viewing through the large picture windows of Joiner's modest two-story country home. Many of the rustic structures found throughout the garden were built by her husband. A treasured family heirloom is a sixty-year-old metal arbor made of found objects by Joiner's father.

By trial and error, Joiner sites plants by height, color, and bloom time. She plants each variety in groupings of three, five, or seven, creating large drifts of color. Over the years, she has pared down her collection to varieties that best withstand the cold winters, hot summers, and wild temperature fluctuations in spring and fall.

In fall, leaves are shredded and laid in the beds as mulch, which is dug into the soil in spring along with peat moss and aged cow manure. The rich loam is sweetened with a light application of lime. A handful of Epsom salts (magnesium sulfate) is scattered around each rose to encourage new growth and enhance overall plant vigor. Synthetic fertilizers are not

Facing page and above: Sally Joiner's garden along Route 8 attracts many passing visitors.

Joiner fills in gaps with quick-growing annual zinnias (below), pansies, and snapdragons.

Several rustic arbors provide a backdrop to lush perennial borders in Sally Joiner's garden.

used because of the potential environmental impact to the lake.

Sally Joiner finds personal and spiritual renewal in her garden and relishes sharing it with other people. Nearly every day in summer, passersby stop and ask permission to walk through, and that, she says, is the ultimate reward.

Invasive Plants of the Adirondacks

European settlers introduced many plants to America. Some species are particularly aggressive and have displaced indigenous plants, disrupting habitat and upsetting the balance of the native ecosystem. Gardeners can help reverse the effects of these damaging pests by keeping them out of their own gardens, woodlands, fields, streams, and ponds. The most troublesome invasive plants in the Adirondacks are listed below.

Purple loosestrife *(Lythrum salicaria)* (photo) is especially common in roadside ditches and marshy areas. It crowds out native sedges and grasses, which provide wildlife habitat.

Japanese knotweed *(Polygonum japonicum,* formerly *P. cuspidatum)* grows along stream banks and forms dense thickets, threatening insects and fish.

Garlic mustard *(Alliaria petiolata)* is a biennial herb that invades forests and fringe habitats, outcompeting native species for light, nutrients, soil, and moisture.

Common reed *(Phragmites australis)* spreads quickly, taking over native wetlands.

Eurasian water milfoil *(Myriophyllum spicatum)* is aquatic; it clogs waterways and promotes mosquito breeding.

Water chestnut *(Trapa natans)* is aquatic; it crowds out native aquatic species and interferes with boating, fishing, and swimming.

Curlyleaf, or curled, pondweed *(Potamogeton crispus)* is aquatic; the decomposed plant matter lowers oxygen levels, promoting algae blooms.

Seven Pines

At first glance, a visitor might not realize that the home on the shore at Seven Pines was originally just the carriage house for this grand estate on Brant Lake. The main house was the large Victorian structure on the tiny island in the center of the lake. The island house was built in the 1880s; a mainland barn, which also served as a carriage house and hayloft, was added several years later. That building was later converted into an elegant home with a wide veranda overlooking the lake. Both houses are now owned and shared by one family.

In 1969, gardens were developed in front of a stone wall that runs along the driveway of the mainland

A colorful perennial border is planted along a stone wall near the mainland boathouse and docks at Seven Pines.

The Victorian house at Seven Pines occupies an entire island at the center of Brant Lake. The mainland building was originally the carriage house.

house. Gradually, other beds were added near the main entrance and at the opposite end of the house.

The main perennial border is planted with a mix of annuals and sturdy perennials. Daylilies, astilbe, and yarrow are surrounded with repeating drifts of annual lobelia and cosmos, as well as modern Wave Hybrids petunias, African daisy, and yellow bidens. Wave Hy-

brids petunias, first introduced in the mid-1990s, are bred for their prodigious growth and exceptionally long bloom time. Unlike many petunia varieties, Wave Hybrids flower along the entire length of the stem, so they can be regularly pinched back without sacrificing blooms. Pinching back replaces deadheading and requires less work.

Preserving a Family Tradition

Like many older camps in the Adirondacks, the Smith home on Schroon Lake has been handed down through several generations. Frank Smith's grandfather purchased the property in 1907 when the region was open farmland. The original camp was a two-story Adirondack lake house that was later enlarged with two additions. The family grew a large vegetable garden on the other side of the road, which was once Route 9. Smith's father, Kenneth, was a lawyer, amateur photographer, and gardener who enjoyed hybridizing irises, daylilies, and daffodils. He built formal flower gardens in back of the house and grew sun-loving peonies, phlox, Oriental poppies, delphinium, and lilacs. He planted gladiolus for its showy spikes, good for use in bouquets. A large wooden arbor from the original garden still stands near the main borders.

In the past century, the forest has reclaimed the open fields, and the terrain surrounding the camp is

Above: The main garden at the Smith Camp

Right: The original Smith garden offered a commanding vista of Schroon Lake. Today the view is largely blocked by forest. Kenneth Smith photo, courtesy of Frank and Kathie Smith.

now thickly wooded. Working from Kenneth's photos of the old gardens, Frank and his wife, Kathie, decided to restore the original gardens. Kenneth had terraced the property with stone walls along the side and back of the house. The walls were restored and extended, and several 150-foot-tall white pines were removed to let in more light.

With the assistance of Schroon Lake garden designer David Campbell, the Smiths renovated the original garden and added three new beds on the other side of the flagstone path to mirror the original plot. The beds are filled with black-eyed Susans, tall catmint *(Nepeta* 'Six Hills Giant'), columbine, and mallow. There are still iris, daylilies, and Oriental poppies from the original gardens. In July, Japanese anemone comes into bloom and lasts for eight weeks. Along the stone wall, hardy shrubs are sheltered from wind and are warmed by the proximity of the house. Sturdy roses including pink 'Morden Blush' and 'Red Meidiland' are reliably hardy in the coldest of winters. On the northwest corner, hills-of-snow hydrangea *(Hydrangea arborescens* 'Grandiflora') blooms from late summer into fall.

Several buildings on the side of the property were part of the original camp. The toolshed and icehouse are now used for storage, and an outdoor shower occupies the former outhouse. Separated from the main house and turned into a servant's cottage, the original kitchen is now a guesthouse. Painted a soft teal, the outbuildings are gaily decorated with flower boxes.

Above: Looking out across the original Smith garden from the rustic porch. Kenneth Smith photo, courtesy of Frank and Kathie Smith.

Right: The original stone wall adjacent to the house was restored and extended.

A Living Legend

One of the most highly regarded plantsmen in the Adirondacks is Jim Cooney, who resides in the hamlet of Long Lake. Cooney operated Northwoods Garden Center from the 1960s until 1979 and again for several years in the late 1990s. He was the head gardener at the Adirondack Museum for more than ten years and tended many camp and estate gardens from Long Lake to Raquette Lake, including that of the Hochschilds, the museum's founders. He has taken great pride in teaching local gardeners the many tricks of growing plants in the Adirondacks that only years of experience can impart.

The Northwoods Garden Center was open seasonally, supplying a full range of garden products and a wide selection of native and hybrid ornamental plants that perform well in the Adirondacks. Most of the plants were tested in Cooney's gardens at the nursery and his adjacent home. The nursery stock was grown from seed or bought from regional wholesale sources. Annuals were bought from Binley Florist in Glens Falls.

The expansive garden behind Cooney's home is built on a slope that recedes gently into the forest. The site was heavily wooded, so most of the trees were cleared to open up the south-facing slope to full sun. Along the house's north side, large-leaved hostas are planted along the shady foundation. Tough deciduous

Hostas flank the foundation on the north side of the house.

and evergreen ground covers and native ferns form a gentle transition between house and lawn. Cooney favors plants that withstand harsh winters and the onslaught of deer and other wildlife that regularly visit.

Hardy shrubs and trees are a mainstay of the gardens. Cooney uses unusual forms of conifers, such as weeping hemlock and creeping juniper, for structure and year-round interest. Sturdy shrubs such as spirea, lilac, cinquefoil, and barberry need little care and are

Jim Cooney's pond attracts a diversity of wildlife.

deer-resistant as well. Burkwood viburnum *(Viburnum × burkwoodii 'Mohawk')* produces white flowers in early summer, followed by bright red berries that fade to black; the fall foliage is bright orange-red. The red stems of baneberry *(Actaea alba)* offer striking contrast to the snow white fruit.

Roses are a delicacy for deer, so Cooney uses few of them, though rugosas and a few floribunda types manage to thrive. The main gardens contain an eclec-

tic mix of reliable perennials: Siberian bugloss *(Brunnera macrophylla)*, phlox, daylilies, black-eyed Susan, hostas, peonies, bee balm, and iris. Cooney's favorite plants are lilac and hyacinth; he welcomes their subtle colors and intense fragrance after the long winter. Because of the consistent and deep snow cover, some marginal plants survive. Myrtle spurge *(Euphorbia myrsinites)* is seldom seen in Adirondack gardens, but it seems to thrive on the warm, dry site of a rock garden adjacent to Cooney's greenhouse.

At the front of the house is a circular bed with a diverse collection of heathers. The naturally sandy soil and sharp drainage simulate the plant's native habitat. The slope continues downward from the house toward the road. At the bottom of the hill Cooney built a huge pond, eight feet deep, and planted it with native water lilies, reeds, cattails, and other aquatic plants. A rich diversity of animals visit the pond, including beaver, otter, mink, coyotes, fox, squirrels, and deer. Several small water features near the house provide the soothing sound of trickling water and a source of bath and drink for birds and wildlife.

Above: Water lilies and other aquatic plants thrive in the man-made pond.

Left: Jim Cooney uses unusual forms of conifers, such as weeping hemlock and creeping juniper, for structure and year-round interest.

A Garden on a Grand Scale

At the Silver Spruce Inn B&B, located north of the town of Schroon Lake, the challenge was to make a garden that would equal the scale of the imposing Adirondack Colonial–style house. In 1996, when owner Phyllis Rogers decided to create a hundred-foot-square perennial garden, her idea was met with skepticism. Eight years later, her vision has been transformed into a bold floral display befitting the grand setting.

Rogers and her husband, Clifford, bought the house twenty-five years ago and opened it as a bed-and-breakfast in 1994. The original post-and-beam house was built in the 1790s; a long seventeen-room addition was added in 1926. During Prohibition, revolving bookcases and secret hallways hid bootlegged

Above and right: The expansive gardens at the Silver Spruce Inn reflect the grand scale of the house. Shrubs and reliable perennials are planted in drifts for greater impact.

Right: From the sunporch, guests at Silver Spruce Inn enjoy this grand view of the garden.

Bottom: Rusty foxglove (Digitalis ferruginea)

alcohol. Downstairs is an elaborate wooden bar from the Waldorf-Astoria Hotel in New York City.

Rogers laid out the garden in a formal grid, anchored with a square brick fountain, and created four symmetrical beds with wide brick pathways in between. Lilac, hydrangea, spirea, barberry, cinquefoil, and honeysuckle were installed first to provide a foundation and to anchor the quadrants. Each bed contains similar herbaceous perennials to maintain a visual balance.

The property is located in a cold microclimate, hovering between USDA Zones 4 and 3. Rogers grows the most sturdy perennials, including daylilies, black-eyed Susan, gayfeather, hollyhock, purple coneflower, bigleaf ligularia *(Ligularia dentata* 'Desdemona'), phlox, bee balm, and spiky stands of rusty foxglove *(Digitalis ferruginea),* with unusual rust-colored flowers on five-foot-tall stalks.

The garden was designed to be enjoyed from the glassed-in sunporch that runs the length of the addition. Guests can relax inside with a cup of coffee or take a leisurely stroll through the garden to a rustic gazebo at the edge of the woods.

The Northeast and High Peaks Region

A Modern-Day Homestead Garden

Route 74, which links Interstate 87 to Ticonderoga, winds along the shore of Paradox Lake, cutting a swath through old farming homesteads above the Champlain Valley. Just before the town of Ticonderoga is the tiny farming community of Chilson, where Lance and Linda Dolbeck settled in the early 1990s. The property is more than a thousand feet higher than nearby Ticonderoga, with winter temperatures often ten degrees colder. Linda, who works for International Paper, the town's largest employer, saw the potential for a garden on the gently sloping eighteen-acre property. Aside from a few rambling roses, there were no existing plantings.

The lawn near the house flooded each spring from runoff that collected from a nearby spring. Lance, a retired welder, installed a dry well to funnel the water away from the lawn and dammed the spring to form a natural pond. The streambed is now dry except during spring melt-off. The Dolbecks built an arching Japanese-style bridge across the shallow ditch and allowed wildflowers to naturalize.

The house is surrounded with lush beds planted with perennials, shrubs, ferns, and conifers. Wooded areas are home to shade lovers including coral bells, hosta, yellow foxglove (*Digitalis grandiflora*), interrupted fern (*Osmunda claytonia*), spiderwort, and astilbe. The sunny west-facing slope above the house is planted with bee balm, iris, repeat-blooming Stella de Oro daylilies, self-sowing rose campion (*Lychnis coronaria*), phlox, and ornamental grasses. Sturdy

The Dolbecks allowed wildflowers to naturalize along either side of the Japanese-style bridge.

shrubs include spirea, variegated willow *(Salix integra* 'Hakuro-nishiki'), viburnum, and smoke tree *(Cotinus coggygria)*. A white arbor is planted on each side with climbing hydrangea *(Hydrangea petiolaris)*.

The soil is sandy, lean, and fast draining. Linda adds lots of peat moss for nutrients and to retain moisture. When planting hostas, she digs a large hole and lines the bottom with plastic bags to keep the plants from drying out. She also adds Soil Moist polymers, acrylic granules that act like a sponge, reportedly absorbing up to 200 times their weight in water. She also mixes the nontoxic polymers into container plantings, which can dry out quickly in summer heat.

An eclectic medley of ornaments decorates the garden, from Japanese lanterns to brightly colored gazing balls. The rustic shed near the driveway is hung with antique tools and a large wooden replica of an American flag. Visitors are directed through the garden by a whimsical sign pointing the way to the orchard, garden, and pond.

Above: Petunias bloom beside an antique-style straw bee skep.

Below: The sandy soil requires extensive amendments to keep plants from drying out.

Antiques and ornaments are scattered throughout the Dolbeck garden, where daylilies are a reliable mainstay. A whimsical sign (below) directs visitors.

Flat Rock Camp

Adirondack Great Camps, the extravagant summer playgrounds of the wealthy, were concentrated around Raquette Lake, St. Regis, and the Saranac region. In 1885, Augustus G. (A.G.) Paine, Jr., moved to Willsboro to manage a local pulp mill. He soon amassed a parcel of 1,000 acres, including three miles of shoreline on Lake Champlain near the Boquet River. The property, still owned by the family, is a diverse mix of farmlands, orchards, wetlands, and floodplain forests.

In 1890, Paine began construction of Flat Rock Camp, named for the giant slabs of Potsdam sandstone the camp is built on. The main house, a long, single-story structure, straddles the edge of a jutting point, framing dramatic vistas of the lake and the far shoreline of Vermont. The remarkable terrain suggests an alien landscape, with an endless expanse of barren rock and twisted, windswept trees clinging to life as their roots struggle to find sustenance in the jagged cracks.

Designed in true Great Camp style, the original

A shade border at the entrance to Flat Rock Camp is planted with modern shade-tolerant varieties.

complex included a main house with seven bedrooms, a dining room, and a spacious vaulted living room at the center. Two sleeping cabins, a chapel, an icehouse, servants' quarters, a carpentry shop, a garage, and other outbuildings completed the compound.

In its heyday, the camp could sleep thirty guests and was maintained by a full household staff. The main complex and several other family homes on the property were sustained by a three-acre vegetable garden, orchards, and a sizable dairy farm. After A.G.'s death in 1947, many of the outbuildings were demolished to make the camp more suitable to modern-day living.

A.G. Paine's first wife, Maude, was an accomplished gardener. Yards of rich topsoil were hauled onto the property to create extensive garden beds atop the inhospitable sandstone. A walled sanctuary to the west of the house and a rock garden between the house and the lake were planted with ornamental flowers.

Along the road to the camp was a large picking garden with raised beds for cut flowers and vegetables that provided fresh produce for the table. The site included a large grape arbor and long rows of cold frames that sheltered tender young plants in early spring. A year-round gardener and several seasonal workers tended the plots.

After Maude's death in 1918, Paine's second wife, Francisca, and their daughter, Francisca "Frisky" Irwin, continued the gardens. In recent years, Frisky, with the assistance of horticulturist David Campbell, began renovating the existing gardens and expanding into other areas. The gardens reflect a more modern approach, utilizing lower-maintenance, sturdy cultivars that emphasize foliage, texture, and multiseason color. New areas include a shade border at the entrance to the main house and a large woodland garden built on an old foundation. Modern varieties of Japanese painted fern *(Athyrium nipponicum* 'Pictum'),

coral bells, astilbe, and bleeding heart are mixed in with old-fashioned favorites.

To the west of the main camp is a four-foot-high sandstone wall shaped in a semicircle, with the shoreline forest as a backdrop. The site, once in full sun, is now mostly shaded and is home to naturalized plantings of hollyhocks, bugbane, and yellow foxglove. Between the rock wall and the shoreline, extensive stands of naturalized foxglove *(Digitalis purpurea)* put

on a spectacular show in June. Virginia creeper and clematis from the original garden clamber over the moss-covered walls. The semicircular rock enclosure offers a picturesque backdrop to the rich perennial plantings of hosta, iris, monkshood *(Aconitum)*, astilbe, and coral bells.

Large stone benches, tables, and a sundial are scattered about the sandstone courtyard in front of the house. Here, the barren rockscape and stone adorn-

Above and left: Expanses of bedrock, known as sandstone pavement barrens, typify the Lake Champlain shoreline around Flat Rock Camp.

ments impart a distinctly Asian feel. A large fountain fed by a natural spring sits at the edge of the courtyard. This water feature supports a lovely fern glen; several species cling to the mossy walls and are kept constantly moist by a steady trickle of springwater.

In 1978, the thousand-acre property was placed under the stewardship of a land trust, the Adirondack Nature Conservancy, ensuring that the land will be protected from future development. The pri-

vate preserve is one of only twenty-six known locations in the world for the endangered ram's head lady slipper *(Cypripedium arietinum)*, which is listed as threatened in New York State. Recognized as a garden of historical and environmental significance, Flat Rock Camp is listed in the Smithsonian Archives of American Gardens.

Stone slab benches and tables are found throughout Flat Rock Camp.

Top and right: A semi-circular rock wall is the backdrop to hosta, iris, monkshood, and clematis.

A Garden in the Woods

Near the quiet hamlet of Keene Valley, a small clearing reveals a garden amidst the deep forest setting. Since the mid-1990s, Betsy Thomas-Train has slowly carved a slice of Eden into the backwoods, blending the unspoiled surroundings with lavish plantings of annuals and perennials. Her log house sits on the edge of a craggy outcropping. On the naturally terraced hill, Thomas-Train tucked compost into the cracks and crevices and planted daylilies, gayfeather, sedums, and purple coneflower, creating a garden that resembles a mountainside meadow. A decorative twig arch graces the entrance of the sloping pathway to the house.

Large tree stumps and truckloads of rocks were hauled out to make the garden beds hospitable. The soil is amended with homemade compost and loads of horse manure that Thomas-Train receives each year as a Mother's Day present. The USDA Zone 4 garden is a work in progress, the design natural, unplanned,

Below: In Betsy Thomas-Train's garden, mountains and forest provide a backdrop to lush borders.

Above: Native woodland plants have grown up among thriving heathers.

Boulders create the structure of the Thomas-Train garden.

and informal. Most of the plants are traded with friends or purchased at Aquidanick Farm in Upper Jay, where Thomas-Train has acquired lots of helpful tips for gardening in the North Country.

A view of The Brothers and Porter Mountains is framed by gardens and woods. The crescent-shaped perennial border sits in full sun, encircling a smaller round bed. Reliable standbys of native butterfly weed *(Asclepias tuberosa)*, bleeding heart, Oriental poppies, and phlox are mixed with more adventurous plantings of colewort *(Crambe cordifolia)*, Russian sage *(Perovskia)*, and rock rose *(Helianthemum* 'Wisley Pink'), listed as hardy only to USDA Zone 6. Towering annual sunflowers define the rear of the informal beds.

In back of the house, an Adirondack lean-to provides a place to relax or sleep outdoors in summer.

The lean-to looks out on a spectacular heather garden planted years ago among the boulder-strewn terrain by Thomas-Train's mother-in-law. A deck that encircles the house is planted with window boxes of annual morning glories, cosmos, zinnias, and pot marigold *(Calendula).*

Perennials tucked into cracks and crevices resemble a mountainside meadow.

A Cultivated Summer Retreat

Johns Brook roars down the eastern slope of Mount Marcy and winds its way through the Keene Valley. Camp Comfort, the vintage 1895 summer home of Wynant and Barrie Vanderpoel, is perched on an overlook along the creek bed. Wynant's family was among the first settlers in the region, arriving here in 1850. The Vanderpoels have owned their mountain retreat since the early 1980s.

The property lies on the side of a mountain, which was blasted to make the property level for the house. From the resulting stone pieces, the builders constructed three levels of terracing and a long stairway leading down to the house. A clearing by the house is surrounded by magnificent stands of 130-foot-tall white pine. Loads of topsoil were hauled in to build raised beds atop the inhospitable bedrock. The stone walls and terracing absorb the rays of the early-season sun, warming the cold spring soil.

In the nearly twenty years since Barrie Vanderpoel began gardening here, she has come to accept the limitations of the short season. The gardens are designed for continuous bloom from late spring until August.

Below: Blue juniper and gold barberry offer interesting color contrast at Camp Comfort.

Above: Hardy azaleas light up the garden in spring. Lilacs, daphne, and honeysuckle add fragrance.

The beds are cleaned up in mid-May, and the soil is amended with rich organic matter. Inventory is taken as to what survived the long, harsh winter. There are always plants that need to be replaced, so Vanderpoel tries new and unusual varieties each year. By Memorial Day weekend, most of the beds are planted and ready for summer.

Vanderpoel, an interior designer who resides most of the year in New York City, is most inspired by English gardens. Her North Country garden is a casual mix of annuals, perennials, and trees, with an emphasis on hardy shrubs. In late spring, the central border comes alive with red, pink, and white Northern Lights azaleas, an exceptionally hardy variety, to USDA Zone 4. Shrubs of varying heights, including lilac, Tatarian honeysuckle *(Lonicera tatarica)*, and daphne *(Daphne × burkwoodii* 'Carol Mackie'), with heavily perfumed white flowers and variegated leaves, create a layered effect.

A favorite shrub combination for Vanderpoel is the bright golden leaves of ninebark *(Physocarpus opulifolius* 'Dart's Gold'), which contrast with the deep burgundy foliage of Japanese barberry *(Berberis thunbergii)*. Tall conical evergreens placed strategically

around the gardens give vertical contrast, echoing the surrounding majestic pine forest.

Shasta daisies, iris, and delphinium *(Delphinium elatum)* thrive in this USDA Zone 4 garden. Hybrid lupines, which don't perform well in the southern reaches of the park, flourish here in the cooler air. Vanderpoel plants individual perennial varieties in large drifts for greater visual impact.

Above the terrace garden, the towering groves of white pine grow thicker. In the transition between open clearing and deep forest lie two secluded woodland gardens with a mix of natives and hybrid peren-

nials. Hostas, maidenhair fern, primrose, Jacob's ladder *(Polemonium)*, astilbe, mayapple *(Podophyllum)*, and bugbane *(Actaea racemosa)* rise above a carpet of sweet woodruff *(Galium odoratum)*, spotted deadnettle, and lungwort.

Facing page: The main garden at Camp Comfort in summer

Below: Stone terracing and steps lead from the house up to a smooth, green lawn.

Marie Reilly with her cactus collection. Courtesy of Paul Johnson.

All in the Family

For Upper Jay resident Paul Johnson, gardening and plant breeding run in the family. This third-generation iris hybridizer's champion bearded varieties reap top awards at local and regional shows. Marie Reilly, Paul's grandmother, began growing iris in the 1930s at her home on Long Island. The family spent summers in Upper Jay, settling there in 1968. Marie created a show-stopping garden along Route 9N, which became legendary among the locals.

The gardens first came to life in early spring, with large drifts of tulips, crocus, and English primroses blooming against a backdrop of a Dutch windmill. The family planted the area's first weeping cherry tree, the arching branches covered with clusters of tiny white flowers above the early-spring bulbs. Magnificent specimens of lilacs fifteen to twenty feet high and wide were completely covered with blooms in early June.

Marie was especially proud of her cactus collection, which she kept on rows of shelves in a brightly lit sunroom. When the weather started to warm, the cactus were gradually acclimated to the outdoors in a sturdy wooden cold frame.

Reilly's daughter continued the tradition of raising irises as well as daylilies, passing on the family passion to her son. Johnson's great-uncle Ed Reilly, who lived just up the road, raised plants for the Lake Placid garden of singer Kate Smith.

Today, Johnson, his mother, two brothers, and a sister all live on the family property. Johnson is a man of many talents: award-winning iris grower, opera singer, baker, and beekeeper. He trained in voice at the Boston Conservatory and sang with the Lake George Opera for many years. In the 1990s, he fell in love with the art of bread making and began selling his yeasty loaves at local farmers' markets.

In 2002, Johnson opened the Standard Falls Iris Gardens and Café, serving up freshly made bread,

Marie started her garden in the 1930s. Courtesy of Paul Johnson.

hearty soups, and sandwiches. Honey harvested from Johnson's hives is also available for sale there. Johnson proudly displays his awards from the American Iris Society above the lunch counter. Patrons can relax in a covered outdoor seating area with ample views of the gardens.

Most of Marie Reilly's old iris cultivars are still preserved among dozens of newer hybrids. The front of the café is decorated with flower beds and planters spilling with colorful annuals. One wall of the outdoor dining area is decorated with garden ornaments, which are for sale.

Above: Garden ornaments decorate the Standard Falls Iris Gardens and Café.

Left: Iris 'Wabash'

Below: Siberian iris and ferns are naturalized along a creek bed.

The English Tudor–style mansion at Wellscroft overlooks a wildflower-strewn slope.

Wellscroft

Near the town of Upper Jay, an enormous English Tudor mansion looks strangely out of place amidst the rustic backdrop of the Adirondacks. Wellscroft was built in the early 1900s as a summer retreat for wealthy industrialist Wallis Craig Smith, of Saginaw, Michigan, and his wife, Jean, whose family (the Wellses) resided in Upper Jay. The 17,000-square-foot mansion (with a 150-foot-long upstairs hallway) was a replica of a home in Scotland that the Smiths fell in love with, and the foundation stones and main timbers were imported from Scotland.

The estate was typical of the self-sufficient Great Camps of the region, with a caretaker's cottage, carriage house, icehouse, stables, sugarhouse, firehouse, and powerhouse, which allowed Wellscroft to generate its own hydroelectric power. The grounds were magnificently landscaped with formal gardens. The Smiths owned the mansion until the stock market crash of 1929. The estate changed hands over the next several decades and was used as a private residence and public resort.

The property was largely abandoned for the last two decades of the twentieth century until Linda and Randolph Stanley, formerly of Lake Placid, bought the property and painstakingly restored the mansion to its former glory. The estate is now run as an upscale bed-and-breakfast.

Historic photos show a formal garden laid out on a flat area east of the house. A pathway led directly from the house to the garden, where a large stone fountain was the centerpiece, with formal paths radiating outward. Mature conifers and dramatic mountain views served as a panoramic backdrop. The rec-

Right: The original garden. Courtesy of Linda Stanley.

Below: Newly built pathways are the beginning of the reconstruction of the gardens at Wellscroft.

tangular garden was enclosed by a low, neatly clipped hedge; a semicircular bench and summerhouse sat to one side.

Later photos show that the garden changed and evolved over the years, and gradually, most of the garden was lost.

Today, there are remnants of the original plants around the house. Virginia creeper covers much of the stonework at the main entrance. Sturdy shrubs and herbaceous perennials soften the fieldstone foundations. It appears there was once a white garden on the east side of the house, because there are still specimens of goatsbeard *(Aruncus dioicus)*, cranesbill geranium, and several unidentified ivory-flowered species. Near the site of the original main garden, large classic urns are filled with annuals. In 2004, Linda Stanley began restoring the gardens to their original grandeur with the aid of historic photos.

A Joy for Hostas

In 1974, Ken and Norma Joy settled in Au Sable Forks on seven and a half acres of land that was part of his family's homestead. The site is a mixture of woods and meadows, with a view of Lyon and Dannemore Mountains. In 1996, the Joys planted their first garden, a long, narrow border of perennials in back of the house.

They were immediately bitten by the gardening bug and soon added two more beds of stately phlox, purple coneflower, Asiatic lilies, campanula, mallow, gayfeather, blanket flower, and daylilies. The gardens were designed to be enjoyed from the second-story deck attached to the house.

In the winter of 1998, a severe ice storm knocked down a number of trees in the thickly wooded area along the driveway. After removing the damaged trees, the Joys had a space with the filtered shade perfect for a woodland garden, so they planted large drifts of ruffled coral bells, hostas, cranesbill geraniums, native ferns, and fuzzy tufts of blue fescue.

What began as an innocent hobby soon turned

into an obsession. Ken loves hostas—lots of them. He appreciates these reliable staples of Adirondack gardens because they come in a wide range of foliage colors and can adapt to most conditions. His garden abounds with hostas of every color, shape, texture, and size: bright gold, powder blue, and variegations of white or yellow. Foliage is crinkled, pleated, ruffled, or smooth and ranges from dinner-plate size to smaller than a tablespoon.

Favorite varieties include 'Fire and Ice', for its white and green coloring, and 'Tattoo', for the un-usual markings in the center of the leaves. At last count, Joy has collected five hundred varieties and twenty thousand plants, many of them hybridized seedlings. The bold plantings of hostas share space with more than 450 other species, including a large collection of Asiatic and Oriental lilies, about 200 varieties of daylilies, and 100 different types of sedums and sempervivums.

The soil is heavy clay, so the Joys constructed raised beds on top of the native soil. A thick layer of newspaper comes first, followed by topsoil and rich

Left: Daylilies and hostas are a staple in most Adirondack gardens, and the Joys have used them to their best advantage.

Above: Hostas predominate in the Joy garden— thousands of specimens and some five hundred varieties.

compost. The latter comes from the North Elba waste transfer station, where horse manure from nearby fairgrounds is mixed with leaves and lawn clippings and allowed to break down for several years. Ken hauls home three dozen pickup truck loads of the free compost each year—a forty-five-mile round-trip each time.

Every three years, Ken completely rejuvenates the raised beds by removing the plants and adding new compost and topsoil before replanting. The red cedar mulch used in the pathways and flower beds dramatically sets off the plants. In addition to being decorative, the mulch helps retain moisture and discourage weeds.

Though hosta is a favorite delicacy of white-tailed deer, the Joys have had few problems. The scent of their two dogs, who regularly roam the property, is enough of a deterrent. ❧

Above: The original perennial borders were built in back of the house.

Below: The shade gardens on the Joy property are a rich tapestry of color.

*A*t the heart of the High Peaks region is the famed village of Lake Placid. The 1932 and 1980 Winter Olympic Games were held here, and the town is a bustling hub of activity year-round. The center of the village of Lake Placid actually flanks Mirror Lake; Lake Placid itself, just a stone's throw away, is surrounded by a mix of upscale homes and protected state land. The Olympic Training Complex draws athletes from around the world with a continuous roster of skiing, skating, bobsledding, equestrian events, and the Ironman Triathlon. Nearly two million visitors flock to the village each year.

The main street, lined with quaint shops, hostelries, and restaurants, is colorful with flowers. Public plantings there are maintained by several local organizations, including the Lake Placid Beautification Committee, the Garden Club of Lake Placid, and the Essex County Master Gardeners.

Gold Medal Gardens: Lake Placid

At 1,858 feet in elevation, Lake Placid experiences bone-chilling temperatures, to −30 degrees Fahrenheit and colder. Most winters, a deep and steady snowpack insulates plants. Gardens in town and along the lake tend to stay slightly warmer, to USDA Zone 4a, whereas gardens outside town are usually in the colder USDA Zone 3b.

In the narrow space beside the Lake Placid Public Library, a lush shade garden is flanked by a double staircase. The deeply sloping bed is filled with daylilies, hosta, iris, globe thistle, and clumps of large-leaved butterbur *(Petasites japonicus)*. Behind the library is a lakeside garden of native plants that are identified with easy-to-read labels so visitors can learn about local flora. Both plots are tended by the Essex County Master Gardeners.

Local business owners take pride in decorating their storefronts with lavish displays of flowers. At the

Native garden at the Lake Placid Public Library

The Great Adirondack Steak and Seafood Company

Great Adirondack Steak and Seafood Company, flower boxes adorn the outdoor dining areas; the boxes were designed and are maintained by local designer Pam Doré. The Swiss Acres Inn, at the northern edge of town, is decorated with colorful window boxes and beds of sturdy perennials and annuals.

Camp Sunshine

Lake Placid has been a magnet for visitors, including some famous ones, for more than a hundred years. Singer Kate Smith, best known for her rendition of "God Bless America," spent more than thirty years at her beloved Camp Sunshine beginning in the 1930s, when she developed a severe case of bronchitis and went to Lake Placid at the suggestion of her physician. She quickly fell in love with the area, spending several summers at the landmark Mirror Lake Inn before acquiring her own summer home on Buck Island. She named it Camp Sunshine and built a closet-size

studio where she could conduct her radio broadcasts without leaving her summer retreat.

Smith spent her summers traversing the lake in her 1938 Chris-Craft speedboat and filled her leisure time with cooking and gardening. The grounds at Camp Sunshine were beautifully landscaped with annuals, perennials, and roses. Ed Reilly, of Upper Jay, grew annuals and perennials to order for Smith in his large glass greenhouses, which still stand. When the weather warmed and the plants were large enough to transplant, Reilly drove them twenty miles up the winding mountain road to Lake Placid, where the seedlings were loaded onto a boat and ferried to Smith's island retreat.

Smith was especially fond of hybrid tea roses, which are not generally hardy in the Adirondacks, so Ed would dig them up each fall and store them in the heated glasshouses until spring.

Smith's caretaker B. J. Cook worked tirelessly on the grounds, gardens, and lawn. Each May, he planted thousands of annuals and a large vegetable garden of potatoes, beets, beans, peas, lettuce, and six varieties of corn. John Viscome, Smith's last caretaker, would carry on the horticulture tradition. Smith was known to occasionally putter about in the gardens. When she became ill from complications due to diabetes, her conservators sold Camp Sunshine to a private party in 1981.

Singer Kate Smith in her gardens.
Courtesy of Richard K. Hayes, Kate
Smith Commemorative Society.

Growing an Urban Plot

Several blocks from the Olympics arena is the home of garden designer Heidi Roland. Her small, narrow lot is more typical of a city yard, sloping down from the level street front to a lower area behind the house. The curbside border is an informal cottage-style garden filled with old-fashioned favorites. In back, a large, sunny deck is filled with containers brimming with vegetables, geraniums, moss rose, nasturtium, petunias, zinnias, and sweetly scented flowering tobacco. Marigolds are planted around tomato plants to repel garden pests.

The deck offers stunning mountain vistas and a bird's-eye view of the lower perennial border. The stone pathways weaving among the flower beds create the effect of a free-form mosaic.

The lower gardens contain lush plantings of annuals, bulbs, and perennials. A cottage-style mix of purple coneflower, delphinium, hollyhocks, and daisies are planted among newer varieties such as purple-leaved Joe Pye weed *(Ageratina [formerly Eupatorium] altissima* 'Chocolate'). Annual cosmos and morning glories are tucked in among tiger lilies and reliable perennials such as phlox, hosta, astilbe, iris, and daylilies.

The site was originally farmland, and the soil is naturally loamy with a neutral pH. Roland is able to make enough of her own compost and collect

Above: Heidi Roland's Lake Placid garden abounds with garden art.

Right: Viewed from the deck, the main garden resembles a free-form mosaic.

Hiding among clumps of astilbe, fishing buoys (right) are some of the whimsical garden art found in Heidi Roland's garden (below), where reliable perennials and flowering bulbs are a mainstay.

enough shredded leaves in fall that she does not have to bring in organic matter from outside sources.

In spring, the garden is filled with tulips and daffodils. One of Heidi's favorite plants is the spring-blooming primrose *(Primula vulgaris)* handed down from her grandmother to her mother before finding a place in Heidi's garden. Many other plants were traded with friends and family.

The garden is richly decorated with an eclectic mix of garden art, including antique tools, metal grates, gazing balls, and even a few round fishing buoys rescued from the St. Lawrence River.

A Streetside Paradise

On a quiet side street near the village center is the garden of Carol Lawrence. The house sits near the back of the property, and neighbors are treated to a curbside display of lush woodland borders and bold plantings of sun-loving perennials. The shade border is a rich study in contrasting foliage, with white-variegated bishop's weed *(Aegopodium)*, blue-leaved hosta, the burgundy leaves of bigleaf ligularia *(Ligularia dentata* 'Desdemona'), and lacy fronds of native ferns. Hostas are a favorite for their range of foliage color and reliable performance.

The beds in the center of the lawn, which receive more sun, are planted with daylilies, globe thistle,

Above and left: Adirondack chairs, rustic arbors, and ornaments decorate the Lawrence garden.

*In the Lawrence garden, bold primary colors
of deep blue delphinium, yellow and red lilies
glow against a backdrop of summer green.*

speedwell, Asiatic lilies, bee balm, and sky blue delphinium. Stella de Oro daylilies bloom over an exceptionally long time. One fall, Lawrence planted more than 200 crocus bulbs, only to have nearly all of them dug up by the many chipmunks and squirrels.

The soil is naturally rich and loamy, so few amendments are needed. The plants are fed a full-strength application of Miracle-Gro twice a month in summer. A hemlock mulch helps retain moisture and suppress weeds. It also deters slugs, which find the lush hosta leaves appetizing. When the slugs become especially bothersome, Lawrence follows time-honored practice by trapping them in shallow pans of beer.

Adirondack chairs placed throughout the garden are painted in hues of bright red and forest green. Whimsical garden art includes a stone frog, ornamental birdhouses, birdbaths, and gazing balls. A twig arbor decorated with large colored lights illuminates the garden at twilight.

Sacred Grounds

When visitors first enter Ruth Hart's garden they experience an immediate sense of calm and reverence. In Oriental cultures, gardens are meant to be a sanctuary from the hustle and bustle of daily life, a place to take pause for meditation and self-reflection. Hart's garden has that effect: It is at once intimate and welcoming. Its personal restorative powers make sense when one discovers that it had been the site of a church.

When George and Ruth Hart bought their house near Lake Placid's famed Mirror Lake Inn, the adjoining property came with it. Ruth thought the open, flat lot at the foot of a short, steep hill would make a good location for a garden. When she first began renovating the site, she uncovered the remnants of an old foundation.

They learned that this was once the site of the St. Eustace-by-the-Lakes Episcopal Church, which was originally built on the lot in 1899 and moved to its present Main Street location in 1927. The long, rectangular foundation and the bases of the stone altar and the bell tower were all that remained. There was evidence that the half-acre property was landscaped sometime after the church was moved, but by the time the Harts purchased the property in 1972, the only hints of a previous garden were a few scant specimens of false sunflower *(Heliopsis)*, Siberian iris, false indigo *(Baptisia)*, and tiger lilies.

Hart felt it was crucial to preserve the character of the original garden and accentuate the natural beauty of the aged stone. She created narrow flower beds around the inside of the foot-high walls and planted iris, daylilies, tickseed, bee balm, and stands of sky blue delphinium. At one end of the foundation, a flagstone terrace is framed by elegant ostrich ferns,

hosta, and hardy rhododendrons. A flat stone embedded in the center of the lawn is thought to be a support for the original church floor. Several comfortable wooden benches provide a place to rest and contemplate the garden. A terraced walkway leads up the steep hill toward the house.

As the thirty-year-old garden became increasingly shaded over the years, woodland plants such as primrose, astilbe, hosta, and ferns supplemented sun-loving varieties. Among the sturdy perennials, Hart tucks in pockets of annual lobelia, petunias, sweet-smelling flowering tobacco, and fragrant ageratum. The naturally loamy soil is regularly enriched with manure and peat moss. In August, the garden explodes in a riot of color from the dozens of flaming red, orange, and yellow tuberous begonias that Hart digs up in fall and replants each spring. She finds the begonias to be the brightest colored of all shade bloomers.

In the mid-1990s, Hart began planting early-spring–blooming bulbs and perennials, which offer a welcome respite after the long winter. Crocus, tulips, and naturalized daffodils are complemented by drifts of yellow primrose, white rockcress, Jacob's ladder *(Polemonium)*, globeflower *(Trollius × cultorum)*, and blue alpine forget-me-nots *(Myosotis alpestris)*.

Hart derives great pleasure in sharing her garden

Left: Comfortable benches are flanked by a lush oasis of ferns.

Above: The site of the Hart garden is the foundation of a former church.

Hart developed flower borders along the stone foundation.

with friends and neighbors. A small street-side sign invites passersby to sit, stroll, or relax in the garden anytime during the growing season. And on one morning each August, the garden once again becomes a place of worship when the Episcopalian congregation gathers for a Sunday morning service among the flowers. The annual service, suggested by a church priest, was begun in 1999 and is held weather permitting. The St. Eustace-by-the-Lakes garden, an important piece of local history, is listed in the Smithsonian Archives of American Gardens.

*Above: The foliage of spotted deadnettle (*Lamium *'Golden Anniversary') brightens the shade garden.*

Left: Begonias and impatiens offer late summer color.

An English-Style Garden

The Silo House provides a timeless backdrop for Cheley Witte's garden. The residence was built in 1890 on Signal Hill, the highest point in the village, and once enjoyed 360-degree views of Mirror Lake, Lake Placid, and the surrounding High Peaks. Now the view is partially obscured by mature stands of trees. The house, which was acquired by the Witte family in 1980, is "Adirondack Victorian" style, according to Witte. Unusual features include a cylindrical tower at the center of the house and two adjacent porches that look out onto the south-facing garden.

When Witte moved in, the property was an overgrown field with the occasional iris and phlox, remnants of a preexisting garden. Witte, who favors traditional English border colors of pastel blue, white, and pink, built exuberant beds along the house and filled them with old-fashioned columbine, hollyhock, Maltese cross, lamb's ears, campanula, and foxglove.

At the street-side entrance, a welcoming arbor is draped with weeping larch (*Larix decidua* 'Pendula'). Just to the left of the arbor is a small evening garden of all-white flowers; such gardens were popular during Victorian times. The light reflected off the snowy

Above: An eclectic mix of garden ornaments, from rustic trellises to gazing balls, add focal points in Cheley Witte's garden.

Below: Luxuriant perennials and clematis vines soften the foundation of a porch that overlooks the main garden.

Witte's evening garden of all-white flowers

The Witte homestead is known as the Silo House.

blossoms casts an ethereal glow at night. On warm summer nights, the air is filled with the perfume of sweet alyssum, heliotrope, sweet William, flowering tobacco *(Nicotiana alata)* and stock *(Matthiola).*

A latticework skirt around the base of the eastern porch supports a host of vines, including several types of clematis and climbing roses. Adding a distinctly Adirondack touch, window boxes made from split logs are filled with annuals. A white picket fence offers a backdrop to the lower English-style cottage gardens. The beds are traversed by brick pathways and edged with rounded river rocks. Adirondack chairs offer visitors a place to relax. Rustic twig trellises are adorned with climbing sweet peas and clematis.

In spring, the garden comes alive with perennial bleeding heart, primroses, lupine, lily-of-the-valley, and false indigo *(Baptisia).* A colorful display of bulbs includes tulips, daffodils, hyacinth, and alliums. Flowering almond, crab apple, and weeping Japanese cherry burst into a spectacular cloud of white flowers.

The soil is naturally loamy, so an annual application of cow manure is all that's needed. Witte recently had her first encounter with Japanese beetles and applied milky spore onto her expansive lawn to control the beetle larvae. It takes several years for the milky spore to multiply in the soil; in the meantime, she cruises the garden several times a day during the worst infesta-

tions, knocking the beetles into a jar of soapy water.

Witte enjoys trying new plants and sharing her garden with others. Her yard and home were recently featured on the annual Lake Placid garden tour.

Adirondack chairs create a restful spot to pause.

Tapawingo: A Lakeside Sanctuary

To visit Camp Tapawingo is like stepping into an-other world. The camp, on an isolated stretch of Lake Placid, is accessible only by a quarter-mile walk along a densely wooded pathway. Even on a hot summer day, the dense green canopy above the needle-laden forest floor is cooling. Visitors find that by the time they have wound through the woods to reach the camp, their everyday stresses have dissipated.

Near the end of the path, the hillside rises steeply to reveal a compound of small buildings. The original cabin at Tapawingo, which is Mohawk for "house of joy," was built in 1929. The current owners bought the lakefront parcel in 1957 and soon began adding more structures. In true Great Camp style, each of the fourteen compact log buildings has a separate func-tion: kitchen, living area, dining room with glass walls, bedrooms, chapel, and bathroom with hot tub.

The camp was designed to have minimal impact on the natural setting. No trees were disturbed to erect

Buildings merge seamlessly with surrounding forest at Tapawingo.

any of the buildings, so the original forest is fully pre-served. The remoteness of the site precludes the use of heavy equipment; raw materials were hauled in on foot, and the cabins were built by hand. The philoso-phy of the camp owners is to coexist with nature, not chop down trees and alter the landscape to make room for man-made structures. If a tree encroaches on a building, the roof or wall is altered rather than cut-ting down the tree.

Nature serves as the architectural skeleton of the camp; trees represent the pillars, and large granite boulders are the sculpture. Visitors can see out onto the lake, but observers on the lake cannot see in. The reverence for nature over the human imprint evokes a

A small outdoor altar adjacent to the camp chapel is decorated with aromatic cedar boughs and red Asiatic lilies.

The deeply wooded pathway to Camp Tapawingo creates a calm, meditative mood.

sense of spirituality in this secluded forest sanctuary.

The philosophical approach to the gardens is the same. The gardens arise out of the natural beauty of the surroundings, rather than the grounds being shaped into formal, man-made beds. The forest floor is carpeted with native ferns, mosses, lichens, wild ginger *(Asarum europaeum)*, and conifer seedlings.

On the top of the ridge, where the main buildings lie, yellow flowers fill vases and pots, a tradition started when a friend brought yellow roses to the camp once a week. On the lower property, by the lake, the color scheme shifts to red, including beds of impatiens and pots of scarlet geraniums. In a small courtyard at the central complex, a moss-covered

stone fountain lends a soothing bubbling sound.

Stepping-stones lead the way through a deeply wooded maze of pathways to other buildings, eventually winding to the lake's edge. Yellow daylilies, species rhododendrons, and window boxes filled with red geraniums add points of color along the shore. Some paths lead over raised boardwalks, giving a sense of walking in the treetops. The stepping-stones are inlaid with glass, pebble, and ceramic tile mosaics. Some are inscribed with messages of spirituality, such as "Gratitude" and "All Life Is a Gift."

At the end of one path, at the edge of a large deck, is a small chapel for spiritual gatherings. Many weddings and baptisms for family and friends have been performed here. The chapel contains symbols from religions from around the globe. The church bell is of Buddhist origin; other adornments hail from the Middle East and China. A small altar is decorated with aromatic cedar boughs and red Asiatic lilies. The chapel embodies the spirit and peace of the gardens and grounds of this cherished site.

Concrete stepping-stones are inlaid with mosaic designs.

Rustic Allure

Not far from the center of the village of Lake Placid, Martina Lussi's garden is challenged by winter temperatures that can drop to –40 degrees Fahrenheit. Her property lies in a pocket that traps colder air. She has witnessed her lilacs blooming two weeks later than those in the nearby communities of Wilmington and Bloomingdale. In fall, the first frost often strikes her garden a week or two earlier than in town.

So, Lussi plants fast-growing annuals and tough perennials that will survive her harsh microclimate. A favorite rose is 'William Baffin', an exceptionally hardy Canadian Explorer rose that can be trained as a climber. Several clematis are reliable here, including the hybrid 'Nelly Moser', sweet autumn clematis *(Clematis terniflora)*, and Jackman clematis.

Lussi's magnificent Adirondack-style log home provides a dramatic backdrop to the garden. Black-eyed Susan, Shasta daisies, and daylilies form a long border along the driveway. The primary garden is filled with

Above: Black-eyed Susan, Shasta daisies, and daylilies form a long border beside the Lussi driveway.

Below: 'William Baffin' roses bring reliable bloom and fragrance to many Adirondack gardens.

vegetables and herbs and has an informal cottage-style border around the perimeter. Giant sunflowers, which burst into bloom in late summer, are favorites of resident chickadees. On the slope beside the house is a naturalized meadow of foxglove, blanket flower, tickseed, daisies, and purple coneflower. The cottage-style design blends naturally with the rural setting.

Lussi uses self-sowing annuals such as violets, sweet William, California poppies *(Eschscholzia californica)*, bachelor's button, and the biennial rose campion *(Lychnis coronaria)* to fill in gaps around the perennials. Lilies, a staple of most Adirondack gardens, are hard to grow here because of a diligent population of chipmunks that feast on the bulbs.

Self-sowing annuals mingle with perennials in the Lussi garden.

Left: An antique mirror reflects a statue of Hestia with a garden backdrop.

Above: Clary sage is one of the unusual perennials found in the Downs garden.

Bearcub Gardens

Some gardeners are especially inquisitive and constantly on the lookout for new and exotic plants. Debra Downs takes her quest across the Atlantic, buying seeds for perennials from Chiltern Seeds in England. She likes the unusual varieties that she can't find in local nurseries and looks forward to trying new plants each year.

Large perennial borders in front of her house burst with color from early summer until fall. Downs's nostalgic sensibility is echoed in her plant choices of old-fashioned delphiniums, breadseed poppies *(Papaver somniferum)*, hollyhocks, mullein *(Verbascum)*,

Tall Scotch thistle adds bold structure and color to the garden.

tiger lilies, and giant knapweed *(Centaurea macrocephala)*. Several varieties of alliums thrive here, including globe-shaped 'Purple Sensation', drumstick alliums *(Allium sphaerocephalum)*, and nectaroscordum *(Nectaroscordum siculum bulgaricum)*, with clusters of small bell-shaped flowers. Husker Red penstemon *(Penstemon digitalis,* formerly *P. barbatus)*, with deep red foliage and creamy white flowers, is exceptionally hardy and self-sows around the garden.

An avid organic gardener, Downs makes her own compost to add to the clay soil and supplements it with aged horse manure hauled from the nearby fairgrounds. From roadside ditches and fields she

Plants of varied texture, stature, and color share the garden in front of the house.

Left: Giant knapweed

Below: Natives such as fireweed are integrated with modern hybrid perennials and bulbs. Allium seed heads (foreground) provide interest long after peak bloom.

rescues plants such as fireweed and purple-flowering raspberry *(Rubus odoratus)*, a graceful perennial shrub with large, grapelike leaves and sweetly scented burgundy flowers reminiscent of wild roses.

Scotch thistle *(Onopordum acanthium)* adds architectural interest to the lower garden. Its thick, spiny, branching stems reach eight feet tall or more, with purple flowers blooming in August. Downs grows lots of lady's mantle *(Alchemilla mollis)*, which tolerates a wide variety of conditions, including shade, sun, and most soil types. Clary sage *(Salvia sclarea)*, although listed as hardy only to Zone 5, thrives and self-sows in this Zone 4 garden.

An avid antiques collector, Downs has arranged treasured pieces on a path along the front of the house. A statue of Hestia, goddess of the hearth, is perfectly framed in an oval mirror against the wooden shake siding.

Although trees and shrubs are not the main emphasis of the Downs garden, a weeping larch *(Larix decidua* 'Pendula') offers graceful structure year-round, and variegated willow *(Salix integra* 'Hakuronishiki') trained into a tree form lights up the back of the border with its stunning foliage of white, pink, and green. ❧

Acknowledgments

*T*here were so many people involved in this project, it is impossible to adequately thank them all. If it were not for the contacts and suggestions compiled by Gail Shapiro and her husband, Peter Fry, this book simply would not exist. Gail, my dearest friend from Glens Falls High School, was the manager of the Hhott Houses in Saranac Lake for many years. Peter, who now works as a landscape architect for the State of New York, was a landscaper who designed and maintained gardens for many clients in the North Country. Thank you, Peter and Gail, for making this wonderful journey possible.

Second, this book would not have been possible without the enthusiastic reception of Karin Womer, Senior Editor at Down East Books. Thanks to publisher Neale Sweet, and to Lynn Karlin and Rebecca Sawyer-Fay, collaborators on *Gardens Maine Style,* for blazing the trail.

I am deeply indebted to David Campbell of Schroon Falls Farm; Glens Falls landscape designer Greg Greene; and Drew Monthie, native-plant specialist in Queensbury. These local plant experts and horticulture comrades generously gave their time and knowledge. To Janine Taylor of Greengloves, who escorted me to some of the finest (and most private) Great Camp gardens. Her patience in allowing me to wait for the best light to photograph is most appreciated. Special thanks to Heidi Roland for showing me so many wonderful gardens in the Lake Placid area.

The historical research was fascinating, with more material than could be included in this book. Very special thanks to the staff at the Adirondack Museum, including Jerry Pepper, librarian; Angela Donnelly, assistant curator; Jim Meehan, former photo curator; and Susan Dineen, director of education. Special thanks to Albert Fowler, Bruce Cole, and Todd De Garmo of the Folklife Center at Crandall Library in Glens Falls. Albert was patient, helpful, and genuinely interested in my research. Hugh Allen Wilson and Marshall Ford of Bolton Landing were unconditionally generous in sharing information and historic photos from their personal collections. Thanks to Sandra Castro-Baker, curator, and Timothy Weidner, executive director, Chapman Historical Museum in Glens Falls, and to Susie

Dolittle, librarian, and Elaine McGoldrick, Adirondack History Center.

Also thanks to Paula Dennis and Steven Engelhart of Adirondack Architectural Heritage (AARCH); Dr. Howard Kirschenbaum; Craig Gilborn, former director of the Adirondack Museum and author of *Adirondack Camps*; Dr. Bryant F. Tolles, Jr., author of *Resort Hotels of the Adirondacks*; Lisa Simpson Lutts, director of external affairs and marketing, Fort Ticonderoga; Ellen Mary Farrar, former garden curator, The King's Garden at Fort Ticonderoga; and Lucinda A. Brockway, for her thorough historical accounting of The King's Garden. Thanks to Robert Bogdan, author of *Adirondack Vernacular: The Photography of Henry M. Beach,* for sharing his photo collection; Richard K. Dean; and Henry Caldwell, for sharing his Jesse Wooley photos. Thanks to Beverly Bridger, Hanni Wenzel, Dave Pike, and former supervisor of public interpretation, Dr. Jeffrey Flagg, all of the Sagamore Institute of the Adirondacks. Also Craig Cramer and Lorraine Heasley, of Cornell University; Richard K. Hayes, Kate Smith Commemorative Society; Anita Richards, administrative director, Marcella Sembrich Opera Museum; Lynn Witte, caretaker, White Pine Camp; Pat Babe, Bolton Historical Museum; Michele Douglas Tucker, librarian, Saranac Lake Free Library; Ralph Cooke, Betty Osolin, and Nancy Harste, the Schroon-North Hudson Historical Association; Marie Ellsworth, director, Caldwell–Lake George Library; and Jim Kammer, historian, Raquette Lake. Special thanks to Robert Hiatt, photo technician at Citizen's Photo in Portland, Oregon, for technical advice, photo scanning, and digital expertise. Thanks to Carrie-Jo Griffen and George Goetz, of Ray Supply in Glens Falls, for digital scans. To Matt Paul for the superb maps, and Barbara Feller-Roth for copy editing.

Special thanks to the Fagles, my second family in Glens Falls, and my brother Gary, also of Glens Falls. To Mark Frost and Sandy Hutchinson of *The Chronicle,* who have supported my career for many years. To Galen Crane and Elizabeth Folwell at *Adirondack Life.* Thanks to Amy Ivy, Cornell Cooperative Extension educator in Essex and Clinton counties, for horticultural expertise. Very special thanks to Barrie and Deedee Wigmore for so much guidance, encouragement, and gracious hospitality; to Robert and Jacquie Garrett, Betsy Folwell and Tom Warrington, Jules and Gale J. Halm, Mary H. Sharp, James H. Higgins III, Junior "J.T." Thompson, Harry Norman, Kathleen Fredrick, Dick and Mary George, Sally Sprole, Connie Cross, and Ginni Campbell.

To all the gardeners who so graciously shared their wonderful plots: Thomas Akstens and Susanne Murtha, Charlie Atwood-King and Karen Lamitie-King, Phil and Mary Baugh, Bob and Betsy Birchenough, Jim Cooney and his daughter Patty Farrell, Peggy Dechene, Lance and Linda Dolbeck, Pam Doré, Debra Downs, Dana Fast, Richard Ferrugio and Claude Belanger, David Forman, Doug and Louise Goettsche, Diane and Tom Golden, Michael and Patti Harrison, Ruth Hart, Dave and Sharon Hooper, Francisca "Frisky" Irwin, Paul Johnson, Sally Joiner, Ken and Norma Joy, Pieter and Arlene Kien, Annoel Krider, James and Jan LaFountain, Carol Lawrence, Bobbie Loosch, Martina Lussi, John and Sharon Marshall, Barbara McMartin, Anthony and Nancy Merlino, the late Sally Millman-Taft, Steve and Sandi Parisi, Kaena Peterson, Ralph and Bernadette Prata, Ruth Prime, Myron and Barbara Rappaport, Clifford and Phyllis Rogers, Heidi Roland, Dr. Raluca Sandler, Dr. Stephen and Kate Serlin, Frank and Kathie Smith, Linda and Randolph Stanley, Sandy Stragnell, Kathy Sweeney, Betsy Thomas-Train, Don and Eileen Valentine, Barrie Vanderpoel, Teresa and Ray Whalen, Hugh Allen Wilson and Marshall Ford, Cheley Witte, and Nick and Daui Woodin. I was most regretful that all the gardens could not be included in the book.

Finally, I am deeply indebted to camp and estate owners who asked to remain anonymous for graciously allowing me access to their beautiful, private sanctuaries and sharing them with the readers of this book. To the owners of Camp Rivermouth, Kenjockety, Camp Woodmere, Limber Lost, Three Timbers, Camp Owaissa, Seven Pines, Loblolly, and Tapawingo, I thank you from the bottom of my heart.

Resources

Retail Nurseries

There are many fine retail nurseries in the Adirondacks. Many are small family operations; all are open seasonally. Unfortunately, there is not space to list all the nurseries here; this is a small sampling. Call for hours. For more information on local nurseries, see www.adirondackharvest.com.

Flowering Meadow Nursery
Michael and Patti Harrison
Glen Road
Jay, New York 12941
(518) 946-7828

Hardy trees, shrubs, and perennials for the Adirondacks

Hhott Houses
71 Petrova Avenue
Saranac Lake, New York
(518) 891-4665

Annual bedding plants, perennials, and more

Mead's Garden Center
361 Ridge Road
Queensbury, New York 12804
(518) 792-6533

Full-service nursery with a fine selection of trees, shrubs, roses, annuals, and perennials

Schroon Falls Farm
David and Ginni Campbell
2002 Route 9
Schroon Lake, New York 12870
(518) 532-9492   www.schroonfalls.com

Extensive selection of trees, shrubs, and perennials, some unusual, all hardy for the North Country; also annual bedding plants, herbs, and vegetables; display gardens; free weekly seminars in summer

Public Gardens

The Adirondack Museum
P.O. Box 99, Routes 28N and 30
Blue Mountain Lake, New York 12812-0099
(518) 352-7311   www.adkmuseum.org
Daily 10 a.m. to 5 p.m., Memorial Day weekend through mid-October. Admission charge. Gardens best in July and August.

The Colonial Garden
Adirondack History Center
Court Street
Elizabethtown, New York 12932
(518) 873-6466   www.adkhistorycenter.org
Open and free to the public during daylight hours; best from July through September.

The King's Garden
Fort Ticonderoga
P.O. Box 390
Ticonderoga, New York 12883
(518) 585-2821   www.fort-ticonderoga.org
Open 10 a.m. to 4 p.m. daily from early June through mid-October. Admission to the garden is included with general admission to the fort.

Garden Clubs and Cooperative Extension Offices

Garden clubs serve many social and educational functions. Community beautification projects, scholarships, and horticulture therapy are just a few of the many projects these organizations might take on. There are many garden clubs in the Adirondacks, including the Carillon Garden Club of Ticonderoga, the Elizabethtown/ Westport Garden Club, the Indian Lake Garden Club, and the Lake George Community Garden Club. These organizations are affiliated with the Federated Garden Clubs of New York State, which lists contact information.

Federated Garden Clubs of New York State
104 F Covent Gardens
Guilderland, New York 12084
www.gardenclubs-of-nys.org
The Garden Club of Lake Placid, the Essex County Adirondack Garden Club, and the Adirondack Mountain Garden Club are independent. Information about their events can often be found in the calendar listings of local newspapers.

Cornell University Garden Resources
www.hort.cornell.edu/gardening
Weather data, latest news, integrated pest management (IPM), vegetable growing guide, fact sheets, and garden links

Cornell University Cooperative Extension
www.cce.cornell.edu
Pamphlets and other information about consumer horticulture, Master Gardener training, and pH testing

Clinton County Cooperative Extension
6064 Route 22, Suite 5
Plattsburgh, New York 12901-0183
(518) 561-7450

Essex County Cooperative Extension
67 Sisco Street, P.O. Box 388
Westport, New York 12993-0388
(518) 962-4810

Franklin County Cooperative Extension
Education Center, Court House
63 West Main Street
Malone, New York 12953
(518) 483-7403

Hamilton County Cooperative Extension
Room 20, Piseco Common School
Route 8, P.O. Box 7
Piseco, New York 12139
518-548-6191

Warren County Cooperative Extension
377 Schroon River Road
Warrensburg, New York 12885-4807
(518) 623-3291

Washington County Cooperative Extension
415 Lower Main Street
Hudson Falls, New York 12839
(518) 746-2560, (800) 548-0881

B&B Gardens

Adirondack Victorian B&B
Kaena Peterson
173 River Street
Warrensburg, New York 12885
(518) 623-2612   www.adirondackvictorianbandb.com

Cornerstone Victorian B&B
Doug and Louise Goettsche
3921 Main Street, Route 9
Warrensburg, New York 12885
(518) 623-3308   www.CornerstoneVictorian.com

Country Road Lodge B&B
Steve and Sandi Parisi
115 Hickory Hill Road
Warrensburg, New York 12885
(518) 623-2207   www.countryroadlodge.com

Saratoga Rose Inn & Restaurant
Richard Ferrugio and Claudia Belanger
4136 Rockwell Street
Hadley, New York 12835
(518) 696-2861 or (800) 942-5025
www.saratogarose.com

Silver Spruce Inn B&B
Phyllis and Clifford Rogers
Route 9, P.O. Box 426
Schroon Lake, New York 12870
(518) 532-7031   www.silverspruce.com

Wellscroft Lodge
Linda and Randolph Stanley
P.O. Box 7
Upper Jay, New York 12987
(518) 946-2547   www.wellscroftlodge.com

Great Camps and Resorts

Sagamore Great Camp
P.O. Box 40
Raquette Lake, New York 13436-0040
(315) 354-5311   www.Sagamore.org

The Sagamore
110 Sagamore Road
P.O. Box 450
Bolton Landing, New York 12814
(518) 644-9400 or (800) 358-3585
www.thesagamore.com

Santanoni Preserve (Newcomb, New York)
Adirondack Architectural Heritage (AARCH)
Civic Center Suite 37
1790 Main Street
Keeseville, New York 12944
(518) 834-9328.

*For information about visiting Camp Santanoni and/or
guided tours, see www.aarch.org.*

The Wawbeek on Upper Saranac Lake
Panther Mountain Road, Route 130
Tupper Lake, New York 12986
(518) 359-2656 or (800) 953-2656   www.wawbeek.com

White Pine Camp
White Pine Road, Box 340
Paul Smiths, New York 12970
(518) 327-3030   www.whitepinecamp.com

Landscape Design

Ecologic Consulting
Drew Monthie
P.O. Box 4052
Queensbury, New York 12804
(518) 792-9557   www.ecologicconsulting.net

Native plant design and habitat restoration

Gregory E. Greene, plantsman and garden designer
13 Northup Drive
Queensbury, New York 12804
(518) 792-5934

Greengloves
Janine Taylor
4 Oregon Pond Drive
Onchiota, New York 12989
(518) 891-0901

Perennially Yours
Kerry Mendez
P.O. Box 144
Ballston Spa, New York 12020-0144
(518) 885-3471   www.pyours.com

Heidi R. Roland
22 Hillcrest Avenue
Lake Placid, New York 12946

Mail-Order Nurseries

W. Atlee Burpee & Company
300 Park Avenue
Warminster, Pennyslvania 18974
(800) 888-1447   www.burpee.com

Short-season vegetables

Chiltern Seeds
Bortree Stile
Ulverston, Cumbria LA12 7PB   England
www.childternseeds.co.uk

Forestfarm
990 Tetherow Road
Williams, Oregon 97544-9599
(541) 846-7269   www.forestfarm.com

Outstanding selection of trees, shrubs, and perennials, many hardy

Gossler Farms
1200 Weaver Road
Springfield, Oregon 97478
(541) 744-3922   www.gosslerfarms.com

Specializing in rare and unusual woody ornamentals. Knowledgeable owners keep track of how plants perform in all areas of the country.

Heirloom Roses
24062 NE Riverside Drive
St. Paul, Oregon 97137
(503) 538-1576   www.heirloomroses.com

Own-root roses; catalog lists varieties according to type, including winter hardy.

Heronswood Nursery
7530 NE 288th Street
Kingston, Washington 98346
(360) 297-4172   www.heronswood.com

Outstanding selection of unusual trees, shrubs, and perennials from around the world

Johnny's Selected Seeds
955 Benton Avenue
Winslow, Maine 04901
(800) 854-2580   www.Johnnyseeds.com

Short-season vegetables

Stokes Seed
P.O. Box 548
Buffalo, New York 14240-0548
(800) 396-9238   www.stokeseeds.com

Short-season vegetables

Vermont Bean Seed Company
344 West Stroud Street
Randolph, Wisconsin 53956-1274
(800) 349-1071   www.vermontbean.com

Short-season vegetables

Miscellaneous

Colonial Williamsburg Village and Gardens
Phil and Mary Baugh
765 County Route 4
Corinth, New York 12822
(518) 654-9569

Open for tours; call for hours

Marcella Sembrich Opera Museum
4800 Lake Shore Drive
Bolton Landing, New York 12814
(518) 644-2492   www.operamuseum.com

Smithsonian Archives of American Gardens
www.gardens.si.edu

Standard Falls Iris Gardens and Café
Paul Johnson
Route 9N
Upper Jay, New York
(518) 946-8328

Sumptuous Settings Antiques and Interiors
(the gatehouse of Villa Marie Antoinette)
4590 Lake Shore Drive
Bolton Landing, New York 12814
(518) 644-3145

Farmers' Markets

www.adirondackharvest.com
www.adirondackfarmersmarket.com

Or contact a local Cornell University Cooperative Extension office (listed on p. 173)

Gardening Books

Cold-Climate Gardening, Lewis Hill, Storey Books, 1987.

Growing Perennials in Cold Climates, Mike Heger, John Whitman, and Kresten Gilbertson, McGraw-Hill/Contemporary Books, 1998.

Growing Roses in Cold Climates, Jerry Olson, John Whitman, and Paulette Rickard, McGraw-Hill/Contemporary Books, 1998.

Trees and Shrubs for Northern Gardens, Leon C. Snyder, Richard T. Isaacson, and John Gregor, University of Minnesota Press, 1980.

The Zone Garden 3, 4, 5, Charlotte M. Frieze, Fireside Press, 1997.

Local Interest Books

Adirondack Almanac: A Guide to the Natural Year, Tom Kalinowski and Sheri Amsel, North Country Books, 1999.

Adirondack Camps, Craig Gilborn, The Adirondack Museum/Syracuse University Press, 2000.

Adirondack Style, Ann Stillman O'Leary, Clarkson Potter, 1998.

A Favorite Place of Resort for Strangers, The King's Garden at Fort Ticonderoga, Lucinda A. Brockway, Fort Ticonderoga Press, 2001.

Great Camps of the Adirondacks, Harvey H. Kaiser, David R. Godine Publisher, 1982.

The Great and the Gracious on Millionaire's Row, Kathryn E. O'Brien, North Country Books, 1978.

Resort Hotels of the Adirondacks, Bryant F. Tolles, Jr., University Press of New England, 2003.